WILEY TECHNICAL COMMUNICATION LIBRARY

Research   Writing   Design   Evaluation   Management

SERIES ADVISORS:

JoAnn T. Hackos – Comtech, Denver, CO
William Horton – William Horton Consulting, Boulder, CO
Janice Redish – American Institutes for Research, Washington, DC

JoAnn T. Hackos – Managing Your Documentation Projects
Larry S. Bonura – The Art of Indexing
Jeffrey Rubin – Handbook of Usability Testing: How to Plan, Design, and Conduct Effective Tests
Karen A. Schriver – Dynamics in Document Design: Creating Texts for Readers

Other Titles of Interest

William Horton – The Icon Book: Visual Symbols for Computer Systems and Documentation
Deborah Hix and H. Rex Hartson – Developing User Interfaces: Ensuring Usability Through Product & Process
William Horton – Illustrating Computer Documentation: The Art of Presenting Information on Paper and Online
William Horton – Designing & Writing Online Documentation: Help Files to Hypertext
R. John Brockmann – Writing Better Computer User Documentation: From Paper to Hypertext, Second Edition
Tom Badgett and Corey Sandler – Creating Multimedia on Your PC
Robert Virkus – Quark PrePress: A Guide to Desktop Production for Graphics Professionals
Helena Rojas-Fernandez and John Jerney – FrameMaker for UNIX Solutions
Jim Mischel – The Developer's Guide to WINHELP.EXE: Harnessing the Windows Help Engine

THE ART OF INDEXING

Larry S. Bonura

John Wiley & Sons, Inc.
New York • Chichester • Brisbane • Toronto • Singapore

Publisher: Katherine Schowalter
Editor: Theresa Hudson
Associate Managing Editor: Jacqueline A. Martin
Editorial Supervision: Barbara L. Hanson

This text is printed on acid-free paper.

This publication is designed to provide accurate and authoritative
information in regard to the subject matter covered. It is sold with the
understanding that the publisher is not engaged in rendering legal,
accounting, or other professional advice. If legal advice or other expert
assistance is required, the services of a competent professional person
should be sought. FROM A DECLARATION OF PRINCIPLES JOINTLY ADOPTED BY A
COMMITTEE OF THE AMERICAN BAR ASSOCIATION AND A COMMITTEE OF PUBLISHERS.

Library of Congress Cataloging-in-Publication Data:

Bonura, Larry S.
    The art of indexing / Larry S. Bonura
       p.   cm. — (Wiley technical communication library)
    Includes bibliographical references and index.
    ISBN 0-471-01449-4 (alk. paper)
    1. Indexing. 2. Engineering—Abstracting and indexing.
    3. Science—Abstracting and indexing. I. Title. II. Series.
    Z695.9.B63   1994
    025.3—dc20   93-30966
                                          CIP

To Marilyn Ward Bonura

About the author

Larry S. Bonura is currently the manager of Convex Press Editorial Services for Convex Computer Corporation, where he is responsible for the editing and production of computer documentation. Convex is a manufacturer of supercomputer hardware and software.

Mr. Bonura is also a principle in Word Workers, which provides indexing and technical marketing services to the computer industry. In this position, he indexes technical documents and teaches indexing seminars to documentation departments of computer industry companies throughout the United States.

Prior to joining Convex, Mr. Bonura held several management positions at various publishing enterprises. In his more than 25 years of publishing experience he has been the managing editing of a newsletter publishing company, newspaper reporter and photographer, magazine editor, and manager of a radio and television studio. He has won numerous awards for his writing and photography.

Mr. Bonura earned his B.S. in journalism from the University of Kansas in 1977 and his M.A. in American history from Emporia State University in 1982.

He is a member of the American Society of Indexers and a past president of the D.C. Chapter. He is recognized as a subject area expert in technical indexing and is a frequent lecturer at conferences and meetings.

Mr. Bonura is the author of several books: *Fruit of a Fleeting Joy; Genesis of the Bicycle in the United States, 1865 –1895; Desktop Publisher's Dictionary; Desktop Publisher's Thesaurus; Convex Style Manual;* and *Ventura Publisher: A Bibliography, 1986–1991.*

Before you begin

What we are going to do

Where the statue stood of Newton with his prism and
          silent face,
The marble index of a mind forever
Voyaging through strange seas of thought, alone
— William Wordsworth, *The Prelude*

Overview

An American writer once remarked that "the presence of
an index means that the author and publisher respect the
book and that a reader will respect it."

A document without an index has been likened to a
country without a map, and it is generally accepted that
nearly every work of nonfiction is far more useful if
provided with such a chart in the form of an index.

Sir Edward Cook once wrote that "There is no book…so
good that it is not made better by an index, and no book so
bad that it may not by this adjunct escape the worst
condemnation."

The task of the indexer is to chart the topics of the document and to present a concise and accurate map for readers. This book will help you become a better indexer.

Audience

This book is designed for:

- Technical writers who are responsible for developing indexes for documents, reports, and other communications
- Technical editors who edit indexes
- Indexers who want to learn more about indexing techniques and methods
- Managers of technical writers who must produce good indexes

Scope of this book

This book will help you learn:

- The function of a technical index
- How to estimate indexing time and index length
- Basic steps for good indexing
- How to select main entries and subentries
- How to emphasize important page references
- How to use the special rules of grammar for indexing
- How to use indexing software effectively
- How to develop cross-references

Using the principles learned in this book, you will:

- Create comprehensive and usable indexes
- Design indexes that work for diverse audiences
- Ensure that your indexes meet audiences' needs

What you will learn

The seven major tasks that will help you create a better index include:

1. Defining an index

2. Determining your audience

3. Discerning the functions of an index

4. Describing the major elements that make up an index

5. Determining the size and format of an index

6. Creating an index

7. Editing an index for content and format

We will discuss each of these tasks in this book.

For more information about how to create an index, refer to Appendix B, "Bibliography," on page 167.

Acknowledgments

Thank you to:

- Lynn Harris and Paula Berger of Solutions, Inc., for their support and editorial comments
- Peggy Gilloon for her illustration help
- Sheri Roloff and Jerry Hill for their editorial comments and suggestions
- My seminar attendees for their encouragement and thoughtful evaluations of this document

Reprint permissions

The author would like to thank the following publishers and individuals for granting permission to use material from their publications:

* Portions of Chapter 2, "Becoming an indexer," contains information reprinted with permission from *Indexing Concepts and Methods* by Harold Borko and Charles Bernier, copyright 1978 by Academic Press, Inc., and from *The Chicago Manual of Style*, copyright 1994 by The University of Chicago Press.

* Chapter 7, "Answering questions," is based on "The user has a question. The manual has the answer. Can you find it in the index?," a presentation, copyright 1991 by Kristen Laine and Janet Anderson.

* The illustration on page 48, Chapter 9, "Selecting topics," is reprinted by permission from *Information Development Guidelines: Indexing*, copyright 1979 by International Business Machines Corporation.

* Portions of Chapter 14, "Creating cross-references," contains information reprinted with permission from *The Chicago Manual of Style*, copyright 1994 by The University of Chicago Press.

* Portions of Chapter 21, "Editing the index," contains information reprinted with permission from *The Chicago Manual of Style*, copyright 1994 by The University of Chicago Press.

* Portions of Appendix C, "Glossary," are excerpted with permission from *Recommendations for the Preparation of Indexes to Books, Periodicals, and Other Documents*, BS 3700, copyright 1988 by the British Standards Institution. Complete copies can be otained by post from BSI Sales, Linford Wood, Milton Keynes, MK14 6LE.

Contents

Part Two   Working with Topics

Part Three Developing the Index

Part Four Completing the Index

Index   215

Part One
Introduction

1

Introducing the index

Index defined

And in such indexes (although small pricks
To their subsequent volumes) there is seen
The baby figure of the giant mass
Of things to come at large
— William Shakespeare, *Troilus and Cressida*

Objectives
In this chapter you will learn:
- The value of an index
- What an index is
- What the functions of an index are

Overview

Readers deserve high-quality, comprehensive, easy-to-read indexes. It is your job as the technical writer to be thorough, yet concise. A well-developed index significantly improves a document's usefulness.

Creating an index requires you to know what constitutes a high-quality index and to understand indexing methods. This book presents the methods and steps necessary to create high-quality indexes for your technical documents. Approach indexing with the same tenacity for accuracy and completeness that you use when writing a chapter.

Why index

Why should you index your manual?

The most obvious reason you should index your book is because your customers want it indexed. Numerous surveys indicate that the most common complaints about technical documents are the lack of an index, or a poorly designed index. Either is a serious faux pas. If you don't think you need an index, think again. Your customer says you do. If for no other reason, include a thorough index for your customer.

A thoughtful index increases the value of any book. It helps ensure that the book will be used often because the contents of that book are accessible.

Adding value

A good index makes any book more valuable to all readers:

- Researchers will not or cannot use a book that does not have one.
- Researchers find a good index helpful in evaluating a book.
- Readers prefer books with good indexes, so they can find what interests them, or locate specific information.

If your document is going to be sold in a bookstore or purchased by a library, then consider these:

- Libraries typically will not buy a book without an index.
- Bookstore browsers often make decisions about book purchases based on what they find, or do not find, in an index.
- Reviewers often praise the index as well as the book.

What is an index?

An index is a retrieval device, an access aid. But it is not a list of terms or ideas, like a table of contents or a concordance, which is an alphabetical list of words in a document with their immediate contexts. Neither a table of contents nor a concordance systematically analyzes the topics.

An index is a systematic topical analysis alphabetically arranged or arranged by function, command, procedure, or topic. It is a reader's most important map for locating information in a document that is read in a random-access style.

An index is one of the most important parts of a good technical document.

Functions of an index

An index directs the reader to a specific topic. That is the primary task of any index. It should enable the reader to find topics according to the reader's way of thinking—it's perfectly okay to include nontechnical words and phrases in indexes.

An index should also allow readers with different degrees of knowledge to locate topics. It does this by showing how a topic is related to other topics in the document.

- Is the topic a subdivision of another topic?
- Does it encompass other topics?
- Is it independent of other topics?

An index should help a reader use a document even if the reader has topics confused, is unaware of an equivalent topic, or is accustomed to different terminology. (Use cross-references to help the reader find a topic easily.) Conversely, an index should help a reader set aside a document when a desired topic is not found in the index.

In general, the index should be completed when the document goes to its first review. This gives the review team a chance to use the index. It also shows that the index is as important as any other chapter in the document.

Planned information

An index reorganizes the information in a document by turning it inside out, if you will. The information has to be broken down and reassembled into its component parts. These components are then collated and arranged in a form at once planned and consistent and, therefore, easily consulted.

Remember that an index is *not* a table of conents and must never be considered one. A table of contents is a summary of the author's plan of the book, how the author has chosen to present the theme in the most interesting and thoughtful way. An index is the indexer's plan of the information given by the author. Present the author's material in the most convenient way.

Summarizing the book

Finally, a good index provides readers with the scope and contents of the entire book in a highly condensed overview, as though the author's outline and treatment were shuffled and reassembled in alphabetical order. Like tables of contents, the best indexes give readers all the information they need on what the book contains. If the technical writer and editor are confident on that score, the manual and its index are ready for printing—and for the reader.

2

Becoming an indexer

Indexer defined

One writer, for instance, excels at a plan or a title page,
another works away the body of the book, and a third is a
dab at an index.
— Oliver Goldsmith, *The Bee*

Objectives

In this chapter you will learn:

- Who the indexer should be
- Who should index—technical writer or professional
  indexer
- Some traits of good indexers

Who should be the indexer?

All too often, indexing has been assigned as a clerical task to a subordinate of the writer or, even worse, to the brute force of an automated computer listing. Rather than a simple clerical task or the focus of a large number cruncher, compiling an index is a creative activity.

Indexing is a complex decision process involving perceptual discrimination, concept formation, and problem solving. Indexers select specific subjects reported by the author; paraphrase the subjects using words that guide to the broad subject areas; select terms from the paraphrases that best guide to them; translate the selected terms, if necessary, into standard subject headings; coin modifications; note the references; and make cross-references where necessary. To make the correct decisions, the indexer should know the subject field, either by education or by experience.

The ideal indexer sees the book as a whole—both in scope and in arbitrary limitations—understands the emphasis of the various parts and their relationships to the whole, and—perhaps most important of all—clearly pictures potential readers and anticipates their special needs.

The job of the indexer is to ensure that every pertinent statement in the manual has been recorded in the index, and in such a way that the reader will be able to find the information sought without difficulty.

A good indexer should also have a sufficient knowledge of both publishing and typography to present the index according to editorial standards and within the mechanical limitations of typography.

Technical writers as indexers

The technical writer most nearly approaches the ideal as indexer. The technical writer knows better than anyone else the scope and limitations of the manual and the audience to whom it's addressed.

The caveat is that technical writers are sometimes so subjective about their own work that they are tempted to include in the index trite, peripheral statements with no topical analysis and, as a result, prepare a concordance rather than an efficient index. Some also argue that because of the author's detailed knowledge of the document's content, the author may be unable to see the trees for the forest and, therefore, fail to select entries sought by the index user.

The best indexes are those made by technical writers who have the ability to be objective about their work, who understand what a good index is, and who have mastered the mechanics of the indexing craft.

Professional indexers

Professional indexers have the advantages of objectivity and experience. While their acquaintance with the subject is not as deep as that of the technical writer, and they may miss some subtleties, the professional indexer is a logical choice for the task if the technical writing staff is shorthanded or inexperienced.

The truth would seem to be that the author can be the ideal indexer of a document, provided the author is willing to master the technique.

Traits of good indexers

Some suggest that it is strange to speak of personality in connection with indexing, and yet the personality of the indexer is never far behind the index. A careful study of any index will reveal something of the indexer's own outlook, especially in the selection and framing of descriptive subject headings. Good indexers have traits like the following:

- **An orderly mind**—It is good to have the knack and desire to automatically sort and classify. If you tend to put your things back where they belong, you may have the right attitude.
- **Wide general knowledge**—Indexers tend to cultivate a large base of knowledge, both within their field and outside it. A good indexer has a level of general knowledge well above average. The specialist indexer often possesses technical qualifications and at least some experience in a technical field.
- **A passion for accuracy**—Indexers tend to perk up when they encounter a phrase, event, or person that they are only barely familiar with and do not really comprehend. This warns them that there is something that ought to be checked.
- **Motivation**—This trait is almost universally stressed. The productive indexer is interested in the subject field *and* in indexing.
- **Dedication**—Related to motivation, this trait may develop when indexers understand that, by indexing and providing guidance to documents, they are making a contribution to their chosen field.
- **A good command of English**—An indexer should possess a love of language, a desire to play with words, and an ability to define a subject succinctly.

3

Technical indexes

Levels of indexes

Perhaps most important, every manual—regardless of its purpose—must be indexed. This is an absolute requirement. And never take the index lightly. The only useful index is one that has been carefully thought out and constructed.
— Gary A. Bolles, "Manual Labor: What's Up, Doc?" in *Network Computing*

Objectives
In this chapter you will learn:
- About book indexes
- About alphabetical indexes

Book indexes

Book indexes make up a large category. These indexes are lists of words, usually alphabetical, at the back of a book. The index reference gives a page location of the subject or a name associated with each word. This index acts as a pointer to the information included so the reader will not have to read, or reread, the entire book.

The principles and objectives of book indexes are a well-defined operation:

- They have a beginning and an end.
- They focus on a general topic.
- They can be prepared entirely by one person.

There is no such thing as a good book if it has a poor index or no index at all. Such books are incomplete and are similar to those books published with errors, like blank pages where text should be, or with an upside-down page.

Book indexes serve several useful purposes:

- Help the reader who must return to the book later to look up some information.
- Aid the reader who wants to refer back to something.
- Help the reader determine if the subject wanted is in a book at all, so the book can be rejected if it doesn't contain the subject.

Alphabetical subject indexes

Arranging an index in alphabetical order is the most common method, since it is more convenient and follows a familiar pattern.

An alphabetical index is based on the orderly principles of letters of the alphabet and is used for arranging main headings, subject headings, cross-references, and qualifying terms. All entries are placed in one alphabetical order, including subjects, authors, and places.

One of the strong points of an alphabetical index is that it follows an order that most of us use every day, like using a telephone book or looking up a word in the dictionary. The only real decisions that need be made are:

- The order—Do you use symbols, then numbers, then letters?
- The type of alphabetizing—Do you use letter-by-letter or word-by-word?

The primary drawback with alphabetical subject indexes is scattering, which means that subcategories of a subject are not placed together under the generic term, but dispersed throughout the index. To overcome this, use cross-references from the nonpreferred term to the preferred term. See Figure 3.1 for a sample alphabetical subject index.

```
Convex, trademark   78
core dump   117
core file   345
country codes   102
coverage, bias in, avoiding   63
covers, placement of   7
cross-index, defined   210
```

Figure 3.1   Sample alphabetical subject index

We will be discussing back-of-the-book, alphabetical subject indexes in this book.

4

Determining audiences

For whom the index works

In truth a very large part of every man's reading falls overboard, and unless he has good indexes he will never find it again.
— Horace Binney, *Letter to S. A. Allibone*

Objectives

In this chapter you will learn:
- About readers in general
- How to determine your audiences

Index users in general

Here are some general thoughts about index users:

- Many who use books, documents, and other texts every day rarely use indexes.
- Many are never taught specifically how to use indexes.
- Because indexes follow different styles, presentations, layouts, and constructions, many users are confused by what they see.
- Understanding and using indexes are directly related to the level of detail and complexity of the indexes and how much effort is required to learn how to use it.

To make users want to use an index, make it a simple task. Users want indexes that are complete and consistent. Indentation, typographical devices, and alignment of headings need to be consistent. Locators should take the user directly to the page(s) required. And, most important of all, be thorough and complete. Everything that a user needs to find should be indexed.

Determining audiences

Determining your audiences is the first task in creating a complete index. Like for anything that is written, the primary audience is the ultimate focus of content, design, and style.

Obviously, your primary audience is the reader or user. But secondary audiences—researchers, writers, students, etc.—are usually much larger and diverse and should be included in your conceptualization of the index structure.

How do you define the audiences?

There are basically four types of readers. Construct your index with all these readers in mind:

1. Readers who need to know where the information is located

2. Readers who may know what they want and use the index to see if that information is included in the document

3. Readers who are sent to find information for someone else and do not know the terminology and cannot read the entire document

4. Readers, such as reference librarians, who must *locate* information

If you create your index with all these readers in mind, you will be more likely to create a complete, usable index.

5

Achieving completeness

The whole nine yards

Indexing does not come naturally, like breathing. It is rather more like playing the fiddle: some learn to do it reasonably well, a few will become virtuosi, but most people will never know how to do it at all.
— Hans H. Wellisch, *Indexing from A to Z*

Objectives
In this chapter you will learn:
- What makes an index complete
- About exhaustiveness
- About precision
- Faithfulness to wording of text
- About usability

Achieving completeness

Achieving completeness in an index involves making a trade-off among the following:

- **Exhaustiveness**—How many of the words in a book should be included in the index?
- **Precision**—How much interpreting should be done in developing an index; how much culling of indexed items?
- **Faithfulness to the wording of the text**—How much should the text's arrangement and wording dictate the arrangement and wording of index items?
- **Usability**—How should the manual be arranged to make it easy for readers to find information?

Exhaustiveness

An incomplete index is almost as useless as no index. Completeness is indispensable. Include every major topic discussed in the document. Cross-reference necessary terms. Give the reader all the means to find a topic.

Most technical documents are not read from front to back. Often, the index is the only way to find information. And it should be the most efficient way to find information. An incomplete index frustrates a reader who knows that information is in the manual but cannot find it. For example, the inability to find information can lead to:

- Customer frustration with equipment
- Customer dissatisfaction with documentation
- More machine downtime to a field engineer
- Wasted machine runs for a programmer

The exhaustiveness of an index can be a quick predictor of the quality of a document. If the index fails to help the reader find items easily, or if the index is incomplete, it is unsatisfactory.

Precision

In addition to being complete, a good index should be as specific and analytical as possible. For example:

Format   20, 99, 152, 166

is not nearly as helpful as these entries:

Format
   default parameters   166
   footers   152
   headings   99
   two-column format   20

Faithfulness of text wording

Beware of automated index programs. They tend to direct technical writers to use only words from the text; they do not necessarily include all the generic terms that a reader might use when approaching the index.

For instance, suppose that an organization uses the word *termination* when shutting down the system. If only the automated indexer were used, *termination* would be the only word that would appear in the index to help the reader find information about shutting down the system. Clearly, the index would benefit from having the following cross-reference included:

shutting down system. *see* termination

Usability

Using words directly from the text without any analysis or translation for the sake of the reader can lead to scattering. Scattering occurs when information of like ideas is put among diverse headings and various synonyms. The reader must know to look in various places for all the information on any one topic.

For example, information on a particular data communications protocol could be listed under the following, which is scattered:

BSC   3-41
Communication   1-1, 1-9, 1-14
Data communications protocols   7-11
Protocols   1-2, 3-4, 5-6, 7-8
Sending and receiving   9-3

To help alleviate scattering problems, use *see also* references:

BSC   3-41
   see also Communication; Data communication
      protocols; Protocols; Sending and receiving
Communication   1-1, 1-9, 1-14
   see also BSC; Data communications protocols;
      Protocols; Sending and receiving

6

Criteria for a good index

Judgment always comes

Isn't it great to be in a profession where you get paid for
having the last word?
— Willowdean W. Vance, ASI member

Objectives

In this chapter you will learn:
- About the five criteria for a good index
- About the Wheatley Medal criteria

Five criteria for a good index

A good index has the following characteristics:

- Accuracy
- Depth of indexing
- Conciseness
- Cross-referencing
- Logical headings

Whether you are an editor, a technical writer, or a reviewer, you should judge an index by these basic criteria.

Accuracy

Accuracy is the most important characteristic of a good index. Without it, nothing else matters. Automated indexing tools reduce erroneous page references, but it is always the indexer's responsibility to ensure that entries are correct. If you are indexing manually, check your page references carefully as you create them. A complete check of accuracy is impractical, but some checking is necessary.

Refer to page 136 for information on how to test for accuracy.

Depth of indexing

When looking at indexing depth, decide what is suitable for the material at hand and the intended audience. The depth of the index should be thoroughly discussed and resolved before you start indexing; once an index reaches the review stage, it is difficult to change its depth.

An average index has three to five main entries for each page of text. A light index has one to two entries per page. An extremely detailed index for a technical manual might have as many as 10 entries per page. Good indexers try to give no more than 10–12 references for any one term, avoiding strings of page numbers.

Refer to page 137 for information on how to test for appropriate depth.

Conciseness

Whether an index is crisp and useful or long and rambling will depend on the choice of terms for headings and subheadings. Consider the following example:

physicians' offices
   full-time personnel
   scheduling appointments in
   use of microcomputers in

A thoughtful approach would achieve more conciseness by using tightly worded subheadings, with the keyword placed first:

physicians' offices
   appointment scheduling
   computer use
   personnel needs

Refer to page 138 for information on testing for conciseness.

Cross-referencing

Cross-references are an index's transportation system. There are two cross-references:

- A *see* reference leads from a term not used as an index entry to the synonym that is used.
- A *see also* reference leads the reader to related information under another heading.

Take time to verify that *see* and *see also* headings are exactly the same as the actual entries. Nothing is more maddening to the reader than a cross-reference loop that leads the reader on a winding path. No index should tell a reader who looks up *memory* to see *random access memory* which tells the reader to see *computer memory*.

Even worse, never refer the reader to a *blind entry*, that is, an entry that doesn't exist! That's the mortal sin of indexing.

Only necessary cross-references should be included. For a subject entry with no subheadings, it takes less space to insert the page references under two different headings (for example, "users" and "consumers") than it does to lead the reader unnecessarily from one to the other with a *see* reference.

A *see also* reference must lead to additional information, not to the same page references under a second heading. Accurate, logical, and useful cross-references are the hallmarks of a good index.

Refer to page 138 for information on testing cross-references.

Logical headings

The ability to select and organize appropriate headings separates an experienced indexer from a novice. Beginners tend to choose everything that looks like a keyword and use it as an index term. The result is cluttered text, with each entry having few page references.

The opposite error is to attach a long string of page references to a single entry, a practice annoying to readers. No one wants to look up 15 different pages to find a specific piece of information. Any subject with more than six page references should be divided into subheadings.

The relationship of subheadings to main headings must be logical. One common fault is to use a heading as both a noun and an adjective. The following example shows the word *acid* as both noun (first example) and as adjective (bottom example). The first example is faulty construction:

> acid
>   acetic, 453
>   -free paper, 12
>   hydrogen ions 175
>   neutralization, 308
>   rain, 15
>   sulfuric, 50

A better solution is to organize the headings this way:

> acetic acid, 453
>   *see also* acids
> acid-free paper, 12
> acid rain, 15
> acids
>   *see also* acetic acid; sulfuric acid
>   hydrogen ions, 175
>   neutralization, 308
> sulfuric acid, 50
>   *see also* acids

Refer to page 139 for information on testing the logic of index entries.

Wheatley Medal criteria

Each year, the American Society of Indexers bestows its Wheatley Medal to the best index that it judges meets a basic list of criteria. Compare your index with these 15 criteria to see how you measure up to a medal winner:

1. If there is an introductory note, it is clear and well expressed.

2. The index is accurate. The location numbers given in the index tallies with the text.

3. Significant items in the text appear in the index.

4. Where related entries in the index are each given location references, these are to be consistent.

5. The index has enough subheadings to avoid strings of undifferentiated location references.

6. The index is arranged in correct alphabetical order or other order.

7. Items and concepts in the text are represented in the index by appropriate, well-chosen terms.

8. The terms are chosen consistently.

9. There are enough cross-references to connect related items in the index.

10. There are cross-references to relate out-of-date or idiosyncratic terms in the text to those in current use.

11. The layout is clear and helps the user.

12. The index is comprehensive (though certain limitations on comprehensiveness may be allowable if clearly explained) and neither scanty nor unnecessarily full.

13. The index serves the text and is not a vehicle for expressing the indexer's own views and interests.

14. If the index departs from conventions, the departures are explained in the introductory note.

15. Abbreviations, acronyms, and the like are explained.

7

Answering questions

The $100 question

What act that roars so loud and thunders in the index?
— William Shakespeare, *Hamlet*

Objectives

In this chapter you will learn:

- How to index using the answer-the-question approach
- That technical documents are task focused
- How to ask the right questions
- About the index as a product

Task focus

What if the publisher of a textbook had to absorb the costs of answering readers' questions, or if future sales of the textbook depended on readers getting quick access to this information without formal reading? Unlike traditional book publishers, this is the situation facing most companies that produce technical documents.

Textbooks, which are expected to be read first, take a reference focus. The index is a road back into the information. The reader is expected to know information. And the reader's time frame is leisurely.

Technical documentation, which usually is used as a last resort, takes a task focus. The user is looking for how-to information. The index is used as a first-time entrance into the material. Time is an issue for the user.

Changing your mind-set

Indexing under the answer-the-questions approach requires a paradigm shift for most indexers. Do think: "What question would a user of this product have that is answered by this text?" Avoid thinking: "This text is about something," which is thinking about the answer.

Identify the task (user focus), and forget the function (product focus). The task is the question (how do I do this?); the function is the answer (by using this function in this way).

Answer-the-question sample

The users of your technical document always know the question: "How do I do this?" For example, a typical user question for a word processing program is:

How do I do automatic page numbers?

If the function for generating automatic page numbers is a subset of the larger function called *running heads*, it makes sense to describe automatic page numbers within the chapter or section describing how to generate running heads. However, if you index the information that way:

running heads, 208–210
  automatic page numbers, 210

you'll hide it from the user. The reader would have to know the answer, which is that *automatic page numbers* is a sub-function of *running heads*. If the reader already knew that, there would be no need to use the index entry to find the information. Consider the following index entries for automatic page numbers. (It would not hurt to keep the index entry above for users who know that automatic page numbers are a subset of running heads.)

automatic page numbers, 210
heads, running, automatic page numbers, 210
page numbers, automated, 210
running heads, automatic page numbers, 210

Anticipating questions

Successful indexes anticipate questions that the user will ask. Most people use technical documents—both online and hard copy—to answer questions. The successful index will make sure that these questions are answered:

- What does that error message mean?
- Where do I start?
- Why did the screen go blank?
- Why does the printer not print?
- Why is the drive not being accessed?
- How do I install this software?
- Do I have to press the Esc key now?
- How do I exit the program?
- When is my data saved?

Another way to anticipate questions is to make a task list that does *not* use product terminology. As you create the index, use this task list as a reference. A solid task list subdivides product into a myriad of tasks according to reader knowledge or expertise. Enlist technical support personnel to review and modify the task list as needed.

Finding questions

You can find out what kind of questions your users ask by studying what happens when they use your product or document. Creating this task-oriented index might require:

- Creating an up-to-date project word list
- Learning competing product terminology
- Performing usability tests to observe what users are doing and why
- Perusing customer-support hot-line logs to see what common questions are logged
- Observing training classes to learn what questions students ask
- Using the product yourself to see what questions you come up with, to learn about priority features, and to obtain an excellent product overview

Meeting readers' needs

To create a successful index, it has to meet the needs of the reader, your customer. To do this, you must:

- Know your customer
- Know your product
- Index under questions users have about your product

Knowing your customer

There are several givens about your customers. They:

- Learn in order to perform job responsibilities.
- Are problem-focused, not fact-focused.
- Do not have enough time.

When customers become stuck, they become unstuck by trying one of the following:

- Ask a friend or co-worker for help.
- Look in the manual for a few seconds, at most.
- Call technical support or customer service.
- Find a work-around or hack it out.

One way to find out about your customer is to get customer questions. Listening to product-support calls and creating a list of questions asked by callers is a good way of learning about your customers. Nearly 80% of all technical-support calls are generated by 20% of the questions. These questions should be indexed thoroughly! Another way to know your customers is to visit them. Talk to beta sites for new products. Go on customer visits for existing products. The benefit is increased awareness of customer tasks, issues, and concerns.

Knowing your product

The best way to learn your product is by using it—and its documentation. Learn the terminology used by competing or complementary products. Develop a task list, those things that your users want to do with your product.

Index as a product

Using the answer-the-question indexing method may require some changes in the documentation group:

- Changing the indexer's role
- Changing supporting materials
- Making trade-offs
- Selling the costs as a cost of doing business right

Changing indexer's role

The answer-the-question indexing method may require that the indexer be a staff person. This person must be familiar with the product and must be knowledgeable about the customer. The indexer becomes the reader's advocate.

Changing supporting materials

To create a successful index with the answer-the-question method demands several new pieces of information:

- Audience analysis to determine reader's needs
- User feedback so important questions are answered
- Task lists to ensure all tasks are indexed
- Category terminology for consistent vocabulary

Making trade-offs

Using this method may require making trade-offs. Chief among these are that the index will:

- Be more expensive to produce
- Require more time to produce
- Demand more investment by the indexer
- Need more pages committed to the index
- Require more work for writers who index

Selling the benefits

But the benefits that result from these trade-offs mean a more usable index for the customer. It also means:

- Increased customer satisfaction
- Increased customer loyalty
- Decreased support costs

Final thought

If your readers cannot find what they are looking for in your document, the manual might as well not be written.

Part Two
Working
with Topics

8

Defining index elements

The sum of the parts

Without indexes we could not easily telephone, order meals at restaurants, arrange for travel, find library materials, schedule appointments, locate correspondence, find streets, or do a host of other things that we now take for granted.
— Harold Borko & Charles L. Bernier, *Indexing Concepts and Methods*

Objectives
In this chapter you will learn:
- The elements of an index
- What an entry is
- What a locator is
- What a cross-reference is

Index elements

An index is made up of entries. Each entry contains two elements—a topic and a locator (which can be a page number or a cross-reference).

Entries

There are several levels of entries:

- Primary entry or first-level entry
- Secondary entry or second-level entry, also called a subentry
- Tertiary entry or third-level entry, also called a sub-subentry

Here is a typical series of entries:

    computer-assisted design 84, 85
    database structure 40, 80
    floating-point arithmetic
      instructions 43, 50
      registers 9
        identification 9
        number 5

See Figure 8.1 for a breakdown of the levels of entries.

```
                        computer-assisted design  84, 85
Complete entry_____↑
                        database structure   40, 80
    Topic (subject)_____↑
                        floating-point arithmetic
    Primary entry_____↑
                        instructions  43, 50
Secondary entry_____↑
                        registers  9
                        identification  9
                        number  5
      Tertiary entry_____↑
```

Figure 8.1   Elements of an index: entries

Locators

Locators consist of page numbers—also called *page references*, *references*, or *locators*—which may include volume numbers.

See Figure 8.2 for examples of locators.

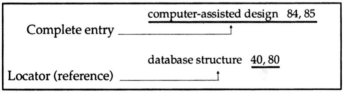

```
                     computer-assisted design  84, 85
   Complete entry _____↑

                     database structure   40, 80
Locator (reference) _____↑
```

Figure 8.2   Elements of an index: locators

Cross-references

Cross-references point the reader to related topics or to preferred terminology. There are two types of cross-references:

- *see* cross-references—Refers reader to a preferred term.
- *see also* cross-references—Refers reader to related topics.

See Figure 8.3 for an example of cross-references.

Complete entry	computer-assisted design 84, 85
See reference	format, instruction. *see* instruction format
See also reference	instruction 29-66 *see also* command; order
	diagnose 32
	test under mark (TM) 56, 135

Figure 8.3   Elements of an index: cross-references

9

Selecting topics

The first challenge

Every serious book of nonfiction should have an index if it
is to achieve its maximum usefulness.
— *The Chicago Manual of Style*, 13th Edition

Objectives

In this chapter you will learn:

- How to choose topics to index
- How to analyze topics
- A quick method for indexing
- About indexing Information Mapping documents

Choosing topics to index

The first challenge in creating an index is selecting topics, which represent information that may serve as index entries. A topic can be just about anything in the document, including:

- Words
- Phrases
- Sentences
- Paragraphs
- Chapters
- Tables
- Entries in tables
- Examples
- Diagrams
- Concepts
- Ideas

The key to developing a good index is to list topics in the same manner in which the reader will attempt to find them.

As the author of your document, you know best the objectives, organization, and content, and you are best able to determine suitable topics. As the indexer you must decide which of those topics are to be referred to in the index and then create subject entries for those topics. When creating subjects, remember that the reader wants information, not places where words or phrases are used. In other words, don't think *list*; think *concepts*.

Analyzing topics

There are several things to keep in mind when choosing topics for the index:

- When a topic explains a concept or an idea, create one or more index entries to help the reader find it.

- When a topic contains the definition of a term, create one or more index entries pointing the reader to it. Often definitions are keys to understanding a document.

- Create index entries when acronyms and abbreviations are used.

- Create one or more index entries for a topic that states a restriction—for example, a caution, warning, or note—to make the reader aware of that restriction. This helps the reader avoid mistakes.

- Index references to place names or personal names that are used only as examples, if appropriate. While many indexers do not index them, they aid in completeness.

- If a topic contains a reference to another part of the document, create an index entry to help the reader find that referenced point.

Because an index is an information retrieval device, index only those topics that may be of use to your readers:

- Avoid creating a list of words and phrases that appear in text. If there is no information of use to the reader, do not index.
- Base the topics on your knowledge of the type of document and the intended reader of the document *and* the index.

See Figure 9.1 for a flow chart showing how to select topics.

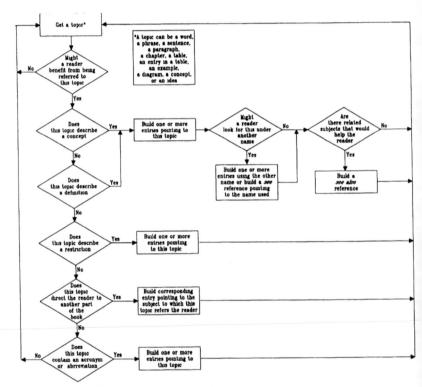

Figure 9.1   Flow chart showing how to select topics

A quick method for indexing

Time-crunch indexing is a method that can help you create an index in a short time. Follow these eight steps to make sure that your index is complete and contains the major subjects of your document:

1. Don't try to index a document all at once. It is easier to index as you go, or a chapter at a time.

2. To begin creating your index:

   a. Underline the words on the page that you wish to create topics for.

   b. In the margin, write a short description for the topic.

   c. Create an entry on an index card, in your word processor, or in your page-layout program.

3. Start by selecting material on the main subject of your document. Just pluck the key topics from chapter titles, introductions, headings, subheadings, and conclusions.

4. Next, index key terms and definitions, abbreviations, acronyms, and restrictions.

5. Be sure to include synonyms for major topics. It is okay to refer users to antonyms, too.

6. Index figures and tables.

7. If a topic is two words and one word modifies the other, invert the words and index the topic a second time, making an entry for each. For example, invert

   secondary audiences

   to

   audiences, secondary

8. Tell readers where they can find related topics using *see* and *see also* references.

Indexing Information Mapping documents

Documents that follow Information Mapping standards are somewhat easier to index than other documents because of their modular format and the orderly introduction of terms.

Information Mapping uses the concepts of a *Block* and a *Map* to structure the writing. A *Block* consists of two parts:

- One or more sentences or diagrams about a logically coherent fragment of subject matter
- A label, which describes the function or content of the Block, such as a definition, example, and so on

A Block is always part of a *Map*, which is a collection of all relevant Blocks about a limited subject.

In most cases, you can take the noun in each Map Title as an index topic and then add selected Block labels as subtopics.

The analysis of each Block already has been completed, and the Block label reflects the purpose, function, or content of the Block.

10

Describing topics

A summary task

A thoughtful index increases the value of any book and helps to guarantee that the book will be used often because its content is accessible.
— Martha Sencindiver in "Taking the mystery out of indexing" in *Intercom*

Objectives
In this session you will learn how to:
- Describe topics
- Select terms for topics
- Create subentries
- Enter terms
- Arrange entries

Describing the topics

When describing the topics chosen, learn to anticipate your readers' needs. Once a topic is chosen, describe it to the reader; this becomes the topic of the index entry. When the index is consulted, the reader seeks answers to questions about a topic. Choose topics that answer these questions:

- Where can I find information about a certain item?
- Which pages can I ignore because they contain information I already know or information I know I do not want?
- Does the information described by an index entry tell me what something is, what something does, how something works, or what must be done to use it?

The value of an index is enhanced when it anticipates the reader's needs and responds to those needs. Such an index reduces the time and effort it takes the reader to find the information wanted.

Selecting terms for topics

Once you've chosen the topic and described it, you must select a word or group of words for topics. Because words selected are abstracts of the topic, they should be as descriptive as possible. Selecting words to describe a topic becomes more difficult as the size of the topic increases. Use whatever words best describe a topic—it is perfectly okay to use nontechnical words and phrases.

Many writers choose subjects from words appearing in the text. Do this with caution. Words from the text are like direct quotations. They are good for those who know the terminology used in the document. For those readers who do not know the terminology, you must provide topics worded so that they can find the desired information without explicit knowledge of the subject.

Advantages

The advantage of choosing topics from words appearing in text are:

- The eyes have something to scan.
- Readers do not have to make any mental substitutions while scanning text for the quotation.

Disadvantages

The disadvantages of choosing topics from words appearing in text are:

- When the word or phrase appears repeatedly, the pure quotation fails as a subject. To overcome this, try combining the quotation with other words or phrases to differentiate among the various occurrences of the quotation.
- Often the quotation is not descriptive enough to clearly identify the topic. Add words or phrases to the quotation to resolve this issue.

Synonyms

If at all possible, do not limit yourself to words that appear in the text. Create the topics from synonyms or other descriptive words.

Groupings

Use common topics as a group of subentries whenever possible. To the new or casual reader, these groupings have little value, but for an experienced reader, these groupings make it easier to select the desired reference. For example, use one of the following terms to describe the topic:

- Definitions
- General descriptions
- Theory of operations
- Discussed
- Restrictions

See Figure 10.1 for examples of grouping common topics.

ABC routine	XYZ routine
data areas used 72	data areas used 95
described 21	described 33
method of operation 153	input devices 138
purpose 3	method of operation 199
reference page 264	output devices 147
	purpose 14
	reference page 285

Figure 10.1 Examples of common topics

Choose whatever words will produce a subject most meaningful to the reader. The most important rule for accomplishing this is to put the major noun or subject of the reference first. For example:

Using *obtaining hardware support* is not as effective as *hardware support, obtaining*, because a person typically would not look up the verb or action *obtaining* in an index.

Using subentries

You must decide whether certain topics will be treated as main topics or as subentries. The primary concerns in preparing the index should be to make sure that every pertinent piece of information within the document is recorded, either as a primary entry or as a subentry, and that the reader will be able to find the information with a minimum of searching.

With rows of page numbers

Main entries that are not modified by subentries should not be followed by long rows of page numbers. Such an entry forces the reader to thumb through many pages before finding the exact information. As a general rule, try to furnish at least one subentry if there are more than four or five references to any single heading. Instead of

symbols 73, 150, 168, 171

you might try the following:

symbols
  alphabetizing 171
  in examples 73
  indexing 168
  numbers and 150

Combining entries

Subentries can be overdone. A main entry consisting of nothing but subheadings, each with one page number, is as undesirable as a long, unanalyzed entry. In this instance, try to combine entries by using broader categories. For example, instead of

    beta distribution
      conditions for   2-29
      explanation of   2-28 to 2-30
      parameters for   2-28
      skewness in   2-29
      use with Bayesian statistics   2-28

you might try the following:

    beta distribution   2-28 to 2-30

Grammatical relationships

There is usually a logical relationship between headings and subheadings. There is frequently a grammatical relationship, too. For example, the orders shown in Figure 10.2 represent a grammatical relationship.

Index order	Natural order
software	
certification of	certification of software
development of	development of software
registering	registering of software
site licenses for	site licenses for software

Figure 10.2   Index order vs. natural order

Grammatical relationships play a role in the wording of subheadings:

- Try to use nouns and noun phrases for main headings. For example:

    finger
    ftp_attr
    function keys

- Use modifiers to reinforce relationships between main headings and subheadings. For example:

entries
  em spaces in
see also references
  placement of
semicolons
  in cross-references

- Use inversion to get keywords to front of phrase, when necessary. For example:

device driver
driver, device

keyboard mapping
mapping, keyboard

However, do not invert:

  — Adjective + noun compounds, for example:
    civil rights
    hot springs
    social group

  — Noun + noun compounds, for example:
    fuel crisis
    reference works
    water power

- Do not use adjectives as a main heading by themselves; usually a noun follows as a modifier. Instead of:

green
  apples
  thumbs

use

green apples
green thumbs

Alphabetizing

Arrange subentries alphabetically. Typically, alphabetize the most important word first. Key words do not necessarily come first. For clarity, a secondary heading may begin with a preposition or conjunction that helps show precise relationship between heading and secondary heading. The preposition or conjunction are disregarded during alphabetizing. For example:

weights
  abbreviating
  of panels
  symbols for

Entering terms

Here are some things to watch for when entering terms.

Capitalizing

When entering a term, do not capitalize the entry, except for proper nouns, acronyms, language statements, or case-sensitive commands. For example:

The Chicago Manual of Style, as reference guide
electrostatic discharge (ESD), causes of
entries, capitalizing
ESD, causes of

Acronyms and abbreviations

Acronyms and abbreviations are acceptable in technical documents. In the index, it is better to use both the acronym or abbreviation *and* the spelled out version. The reference *ESD, causes of,* should also be listed under *electrostatic discharge (ESD), causes of.*

If you choose to use only the spelled out version of acronyms and synonyms, create a cross-reference (*see*) from the acronym or synonym to the spelled out version. Place the acronym or synonym in parentheses after the spelled out version. For example:

    electrostatic discharge (ESD)
      causes of 29
      preventing 45
    ESD. *see* electrostatic discharge (ESD)

Jargon

Avoid jargon. If you wish to index jargon, enter the word and use a cross-reference to point to the more commonly accepted entry.

Singular vs. plural

It is okay to use either the singular or plural; just be consistent. Uniformity—in spelling, plurality, and description—is required to keep subjects together in the index to prevent them from being scattered.

11

Arranging topics

Putting entries in order

Far from being the easiest and most numbingly uncreative part of writing a document, the index is a painstaking and difficult task. It's also impossible with the software that now exists. There isn't one piece of software that can do the job, so my only real recommendation must be, if you need an index, get an indexer (a human one) to do it.
— William Gallagher in "Indicing with death" in *Personal Computer World*

Objectives

In this session you will learn how to:

- Arrange entries for emphasis
- Beware of factoring
- Use economies of size

Using emphasis

Always arrange entries for emphasis. Place the most important word first if readability is not adversely affected. Base your word arrangement decisions on the purpose of the document and its audience.

See Figure 11.1 for an arrangement of words for emphasis.

Arrangement A	Arrangement B
control statements	control statements
comments	comments
parameters	parameters
format of input	input, format of
format of output	input, use of
storage of	output, format of
use of defaults	output, use of
use of input	storage of
use of output	use of defaults

Figure 11.1 Arranging words for emphasis

Beware of factoring

When grouping entries, beware of *factoring*, which is the process of dividing groups of words so that the meanings are changed. Factoring is an illogical placement of entries in false categories and makes users go through additional steps to find a topic. Misuse of factoring will mislead and confuse the reader. To reduce factoring, do not use an adjective alone as the subject of a primary entry.

See Figure 11.2 for an example of factoring as part of word grouping.

Potential Entries	Grouped Entries
binary operator	operator
logical AND operator	binary
logical OR operator	logical AND
messages to operator	logical OR
unary operator	unary
	operator, messages to

Figure 11.2 Factoring as part of word grouping

Using economies of size

You can use certain economies of size without detriment to the index. One of the most usual economies is combining topics and the operations associated with them. For example, in a book on finance, there may be several references to banks, and several more to the practice of banking. If there are a large number of references to both, make separate references; but if there are only a few, consider whether these two could safely be combined under the one heading. For example:

computing   56, 69
computers   58, 68

can be combined into

computers and computing   56, 58, 68, 69

12

Handling special cases

Things to watch for

...[Thomas] Jefferson was an inveterate indexer; he indexed account books, journals, and memorandum books. Making lists, classifying, ordering, collecting, and saving were symptoms of his compulsive personality. Indexing was not merely utilitarian; it was a necessity.
— Jack McLaughlin in "The Organized President" in *American Heritage*

Objectives

In this chapter you will learn how to index:
- Restrictions
- Definitions
- Acronyms and abbreviations
- References to other publications
- Numbers and symbols

Restrictions

The reader must be able to find all restrictions and the index should make the reader aware of them. Do not just list the restriction. Be sure to describe it, too. There are several types of restrictions that should be indexed:

- Sets of rules
- Default values or options
- Warnings
- Cautions
- Notes

Definitions

While glossaries do not have to be indexed, sometimes it helps the reader if the glossary is indexed. It would be a good habit to index all definitions, those in the glossary as well as in text. If the definition appears in the text and glossary, each with slight variations in meaning, you might show the differences in the index by choosing a term that is used consistently to define each. For example:

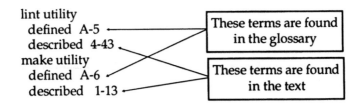

lint utility
    defined A-5
    described 4-43
make utility
    defined A-6
    described 1-13

These terms are found in the glossary

These terms are found in the text

In this example, each time a topic in the glossary was indexed, the term *defined* was used. When the same topic was described in text, the term *described* was used.

Acronyms and abbreviations

Placing acronyms and abbreviations in the index lets the reader know whether or not the information represented by the acronym or abbreviation is in the document. For example:

CPU. *see* central processing unit (CPU)

At the spelled-out term, place the abbreviation at the end of the term. For example:

central processing unit (CPU)

Such entries often refresh a reader's memory.

Referring to other publications

If the document being indexed is a continuation of a prerequisite or co-requisite publication, you may provide index entries to other publications to ensure that a reader can proceed easily from that document to your document and vice versa.

Let's say you are producing an index for *ABC Manual*. A previous book, *XYZ Manual*, contains the following statement in several places:

Refer to *ABC Manual* for a listing and description of the conversion programs.

In *ABC Manual*, each conversion program was given a specific name. If the names of the conversion programs appeared in the index only under the specific names, the reader of *XYZ Manual* would not find them. While creating index entries for *ABC Manual*, provide for the reader who will be looking for "conversion programs":

conversion programs
  aconvert 40
  bconvert 80
  cconvert 100

Numeric and symbol subjects

While it is best to place numeric and symbol entries in the numeric and symbol portions of the index, it is perfectly okay to place them under headings as if they were spelled out. Symbols usually precede numerals when placed together, and both come under separate letter headings. Here is an example of symbols and numerals being placed under the symbols and numerals heading:

Symbols
!, repeat command
&, for background operation
+, Boolean operator

Numerals
286
386
486

Here are those same symbols and numerals placed as if spelled out:

A
ampersand (&), for background operation

E
exclamation point (!), for repeat command

F
486 (four eighty-six)

P
plus sign (+), Boolean operator

T
386 (three eighty-six)
286 (two eighty-six)

13

Alphabetizing the index

The arrangement of entries

The letter-by-letter system tends to make alphabetizing a little easier for the indexer, while the word-by-word system can be easier for the reader because it groups identical single words together. But the differences are minor, and either system can, at times, result in an awkward-looking series.
— *Webster's Standard American Style Manual*

Objectives
In this chapter you will learn:
- How to alphabetize your index
- What letter-by-letter alphabetizing is
- What word-by-word alphabetizing is
- The alphabetizing order of entries

Alphabetizing methods

There are two primary methods of alphabetization:

- Letter-by-letter
- Word-by-word

Actually, all alphabetizing is letter-by-letter because readers consider first the initial letter of the word, then the second letter, then the third, and so on. The need to choose between the two methods arises when you alphabetize not a set of single words, but a set of headings, some of which consist of more than one word.

See Figure 13.1 for a comparison of letter-by-letter and word-by-word alphabetization.

Letter-by-Letter	Word-by-Word
olden	Old English
Old English	old-fashioned
oldfangled	Old Glory
old-fashioned	old hand
Old Glory	Old Irish
old hand	old lady
oldie	old wives' tale
Old Irish	olden
oldish	oldfangled
old lady	oldie
oldster	oldish
oldwife	oldster
old wives' tale	oldwife

Figure 13.1   Letter-by-letter vs. word-by-word alphabetizing

Letter-by-letter

In the letter-by-letter method, alphabetize up to the first punctuation mark. That is, ignore word spaces and alphabetize up to the hyphen, comma, colon, or period at the end of the heading, or to the comma after the first part of the inverted heading (see Figure 13.1).

Word-by-word

In the word-by-word method, alphabetize through the end of the first word, then stop. Use second and subsequent words only when two or more headings begin with the same word or words (see Figure 13.1). If there is a hyphen separating the words, treat the words as individual elements.

Choosing one or the other

Each system has its pros and cons. Adherents of the word-by-word method say that the letter-by-letter system is easy on the indexer and hard on the reader. Detractors of the word-by-word method say that everyone is familiar with a dictionary and, therefore, is fully familiar with the letter-by-letter method. In either case, both are acceptable, with the letter-by-letter method being more popular.

Alphabetizing order

When you alphabetize, use this sequence:
- Symbols, punctuation, and special characters
- Numerals
- Uppercase letters
- Lowercase letters

Computers alphabetize according to their ASCII decimal code number. For example, the exclamation point (!) is always alphabetized first because it has the lowest ASCII decimal code. Numbers alphabetize before letters. Uppercase letters alphabetize before lowercase letters.

You can place symbols, special characters, punctuation, and numbers in the letter grouping for their names instead of under the symbol, number, punctuation, or special character. For example, place the entry for an * under *asterisk (*)* rather than under the symbol *. And place the entry for *64,000* under *sixty-four thousand* rather than under the number heading.

Part Three
Developing
the Index

14

Creating
cross-references

See *and* see also

The index is the most important finding tool a publication
can provide. It should be extensive, going well beyond the
glossary and table of contents.... Cross-references must be
correct and complete.
— *Xerox Publishing Standards*

Objectives
In this chapter you will learn:
- How to create cross-references
- How to create *see* references
- How to create *see also* references
- Where to place *see also* references

Creating cross-references

Cross-references in the index guide the reader to related information in the document. Properly used, they are helpful adjuncts to an index, but they should never be used unless they actually lead to additional information, not just the same information indexed under other headings. While cross-references are usually *italicized*, the only time they are usually not italicized is when used in a cross-reference that is also italicized. For example:

The Chicago Manual of Style. see *Chicago Manual of Style*

In cross-referencing, headings and subheadings are usually cited in full, with inversion and punctuation exactly as given in the entry referenced. For example:

electrostatic discharge (ESD), 334–338
  see also humidity
humidity, 176
  see also electrostatic discharge (ESD)

Exceptions are sometimes made, however, for very long headings. When multiple principal headings are cited, these should be separated by semicolons. Multiple cross-references are arranged in alphabetical order. For example:

elisions, 34
  see also inclusive numbers; locators

If the reference is to a subheading, its principal heading should be given first, followed by a colon or a comma and then the subheading. For example:

electrostatic discharge (ESD)
    static prevention, 3-12 to 3-24, 6-156
static prevention. *see* electrostatic discharge (ESD), static
    prevention

Cross-references are used in place of a page reference, or *locator*. Use cross-references sparingly, but don't skimp on them just to keep the index short. As always, the main criterion for using cross-references is completeness.

Cross-references take two general forms:

- *See* references
- *See also* references

See references

Use *see* references in the following situations:

- When the writer has chosen one among several key words or phrases and the reader might look under another, for example:

  virgule. *see* slash

- When the subject has been treated as a subentry to a principal entry, for example:

  Iroquois Indians. *see* Indian tribes, Iroquois

- When an entry has been alphabetized under another letter of the alphabet, for example:

  Hague. *see* The Hague

Guard against a *blind entry*, which is a cross-reference to an entry that is not listed in the index. Using the first bullet example above, if you list *virgule* as a cross-reference and point the reader to *slash* as the term under which you list entries to *virgule*, then make sure you have included *slash* as a primary entry. If you don't, you have created a blind entry.

While *see* references are usually italicized when used in indexes, the only time they are usually not italicized is when used in a cross-reference that is also italicized.

The *see* reference immediately follows the referenced word.

Some indexers do not use *see* references. Rather, they place page numbers at both subjects, using parentheses to indicate alternative usages. See Figure 14.1 for an alternative to using *see* references.

```
access mechanism (comb)  15
comb (access mechanism)  15
core (main storage)
    addressing  40
    allocation of  60
main storage (memory)
    addressing  40
    allocation of  60
memory (main storage)
    addressing  40
    allocation of  60
```

Figure 14.1 Alternative to using *see* references

Parentheses are also used to differentiate homonyms,
which are people or things with identical names. For
example:

screen (computer)
screen (to cover)

See also references

See also references are used when additional or related information can be found in another entry or subentry. See Figure 14.2 for examples of *see also* references.

These entries point out related information

air flow
    see also thermal circuit breaker
heat sink
    see also power transistors
power transistors
    see also heat sink
thermal circuit breaker
    see also air flow

These entries suggest alternatives that would not have occurred to the reader

PCONVERT routine
    see also standalone conversion routine
standalone conversion routine
    see also PCONVERT routine

Figure 14.2   Examples of *see also* references

A *see also* reference is an aid to help the reader use the index. It points out related information, identifies subjects similar in form or purpose, or suggests alternatives or equivalents if the reader's first choice is wrong.

While *see also* references are usually italicized when used in indexes, the only time they are usually not italicized is when used in a cross-reference that is also italicized.

Where to place the *see also*

Place your *see also* cross-reference in one of four locations:

- Immediately below the main heading
- As the last subheading entry
- Immediately to the right of the main heading
- At the end of the page references

Where you place the *see also* reference is your choice. However, most indexers place it right below the main heading to let the reader immediately know that there is a related term. This is usually done to prevent the user from going through the list of entries to find that the subject really sought is somewhere else.

Below the main heading

In this location, the *see also* cross-reference is the first subheading entry. For example:

Churches
   see also Constantine; orders, religious
   Roman 273–275
   Romanesque 309, 324, 542

As the last subheading

In this location, the *see also* cross-reference is the last subheading entry. For example:

Churches
   Roman 273–275
   Romanesque 309, 324, 542
   see also Constantine; orders, religious

To the right of the main heading

In this location, the *see also* cross-reference is placed to the right of the main heading, usually in parentheses. For example:

Churches
 Roman (*see also* Constantine) 273–275
 Romanesque (*see also* order, religious) 309, 324, 542

At the end of the page references

In this location, the *see also* cross-reference is placed at the end of the page references. For example:

Churches
 Roman 273–275. *see also* Constantine
 Romanesque 309, 324, 542. *see also* order, religious

Electronic file placement

Here's a great tip on where to place your cross-references when using computer files. Place all *see* and *see also* references in one place—like at the end of the preface or chapter one. It is easier to find the terms this way if you need to edit them. If you scatter the cross-references throughout the files, you will have a difficult time locating the one you need to edit.

15

Working with locators

Please turn to page 3

The *Index Expurgatorius* issued by Pope Sixtus V in 1589 states in its Rule XXI: "Not only shall be expurgated books, but also marginal notes, obscene pictures, indexes, letters, prefaces, and everything the book contains."
— William Popper, *The Censorship of Hebrew Books*

Objectives
In this chapter you will learn how to record:
- Locators
- Inclusive numbers
- Nontext references

Recording locators

The term *locator* is used instead of page reference because not all references are page numbers. Sometimes references are made to divisions of books, such as chapters, sections, subsections, or paragraphs.

Observe the following procedures to record locators:

- Verify the page number immediately; be sure that it is accurate.
- Give comprehensive page numbers for locating continuous treatment of the subject. For example:
  116–117
  3-1 to 3-9

- Do not use continuous page numbers for locating separate occurrences of a subject; record each page separately. If there are three items having the same subject and modifications on successive pages, record them that way. For example:
  73, 74, 75 *not* 73–75

  If you use the 73–75 reference, it indicates to the reader that the reference is to a 3-page continuous discussion.

- If repetitions of the same modification occur on a sizable number of pages in close proximity—53, 54, 55, 57, 58, 60, 61—the references may be collected. For example:
  53–61, mentioned

  This approach does not mislead the reader, but provides an adequate guide and has the advantage of economy of space.

- Page numbers for matter in footnotes falling on pages of text should show that the references are to notes. For example:

54 n

where there is a thin space between the page number and the n. For multiple footnote references use the page number with an "nn." (note the period) followed by the footnote numbers. For example:

54 nn. 17, 18

- In those instances where you have hyphens in your page references, it's much easier to see the range if you use the word "to" rather than an em dash or a hyphen to show a range of pages. For example:

3-54 to 3-56

not

3-54–3-56

Locators are always separated by commas and are always in numerical sequence from lowest to highest or in alphabetical order.

Inclusive numbers

Inclusive page numbers tell readers where topics begin, are interrupted, and continue. If the topic discussed runs on continuous pages, the pages should be linked with an en dash:

24–25

If the references are two separate, discontinuous ones, the page numbers are separated by commas:

24, 25

For example, the references

212–216, 219–220, 222

indicate that there is a lengthy discussion of the topic on pages 212 through 216, with a shorter mention on pages 219 through 220 and a brief mention on page 222.

Styles for inclusive numbers

There are two ways to present inclusive numbers:

1. Put numbers in full: 232–234, 504–506, 3-6 to 3-9
2. Elide the numbers: 232–34, 504–6

Rules for using elisions

If you decide to use elision of inclusive numbers, follow these rules:

1. Do not elide inclusive numbers that have only two digits: 33–37, not 33–7.

2. Do not elide inclusive numbers when the first number ends in 00: 100–108, not 100–08 and not 100–8.

3. In other numbers, omit only the hundreds digits from the higher number: 232–34, not 232–4.

4. Where the next-to-last digit of both numbers is zero, write only one digit for the higher number: 103–4, not 103–04.

5. Do not use elision on locators using chapter-page number ranges: 3-6 to 3-9, not 3-6 to 9 or 3-6–9.

Nontext references

Nontext materials such as tables, charts, photographs, maps, diagrams, and other illustrations are sometimes identified as such in indexes. One way to identify illustrations is to print in italic or boldface type any numbers that locate such material. If you use this method, you need to add a note at the beginning of the index to explain the procedure. For example:

Note: Boldface numbers refer to photographs; italic numbers refer to tables.

back plane, 33–50, *45*
chemical notation, 101, **102**

Another method is for the locator numbers to be preceded by an identifying term such as *map, table, illus.* in italic. These special locators may be positioned at the end of the regular numbers. For example:

power supply   25–28, 67, *illus.* 54

They may also be placed in sequence with other locators, which is the more common practice. For example:

power supply   25–28, *illus.* 54, 67

Some indexers prefer to list illustrations as separate subheadings to make them more obvious. For example:

networks
  backing up   44–45
  configuring   23, 68
    illustrated   24

16

Preparing index cards

The mechanics

When Andy Warhol's biography came out…, without an index, a Warner Books spokesperson reportedly defended the move by saying, "We felt the book should be read as a complete body of work."…Several magazines, including *Spy* and *Fame*, made up for the lack by devising their own indexes and creating entries such as 'Ono, Yoko, greed of' and 'Ross, Diana, ugliness of in *The Wiz*'.
— Martin R. Dowding, *Books in Canada*

Objectives
In this chapter you will learn how to:
- Use index cards
- Mark entries on index cards
- Transfer entries to index cards
- Arrange the index cards
- Edit the index cards
- Mark the index cards for typing

Starting place

An excellent way to start indexing is to do it using the shoe box method. Use index cards to record your entries. Put them all into a shoe box and then alphabetize and edit them. This will give you a good feel for how the mechanics are done—whether with a standalone indexing program or desktop publishing package.

Using index cards

Each index entry is recorded on a separate 3-inch by 5-inch index card. Use these cards to prepare the final index. If you are using a computer, word processor, or desktop publishing program, change or adapt the procedures discussed in this chapter as necessary to reflect the capabilities of your particular system.

Marking entries

On your page proof, underline or circle topics that should be included in the index. If the exact word or phrase that is wanted for the index does not appear in the text, write the exact wording in the margin of the proof. This marking is for your convenience, do as much or as little of it as you find necessary.

Transferring entries to cards

After marking your entries on the page proofs, copy the
index items on 3-inch by 5-inch cards. Use a separate card
for each main entry and subentry, repeating the main entry
at the top of each card. This is done for convenience and
accuracy in the final arrangements of the index. Every card
has two or three elements on it: a heading, a modification
(if necessary), and a locator. The cards should look like
those shown in Figure 16.1.

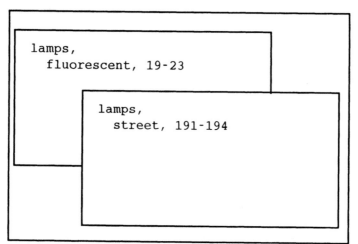

```
lamps,
    fluorescent, 19-23
```

```
lamps,
    street, 191-194
```

Figure 16.1 Example of index cards for two subentries

Every time you make a card, reread what you have written
and verify the page number. Once cards have been put in
alphabetical order, it will be difficult or impossible to
correct miscopied page numbers.

For novice indexers, it would be best to keep the cards in
the order in which you made them until you have finished
making cards for the entire document. This means that you
will not be able to add new page numbers to cards you
have already made; but the added work is justified by the
advantage of being able to check all cards against the pages
they refer to before they are reshuffled in alphabetizing.

When all the cards are completed, go through the file once more with the page proofs at your side and do two things:

1. Check each card to make sure that what is on its face is exactly what you intended.

2. Go through the page proofs once more to check for omissions in the indexing. Previously unmarked items may have proved to be indexable in the light of themes developed in later chapters.

In each case, make cards now and add them to the file before alphabetizing.

While the making of the index will be slow at the beginning, owing to the necessity of writing many cards, it will gradually become quicker as less and less headings have to be written, and the work becomes mainly one of adding aspects and page references to the existing cards. To this end, it is wise to add references from synonymous headings as soon as they come to mind, to avoid waste of effort in making duplicate entries under different headings.

It will be found, generally speaking, that while the indexer will usually remember the headings used during the first 20 to 30 pages, the indexer's memory will not always record them all during the subsequent indexing, especially if this takes place over a lengthy period. Making references, in writing, from synonymous headings will help turn the indexer to the main headings that have been decided upon previously. If these are not recorded, the indexer may find scattering deficiencies in the index.

Arranging the cards

Alphabetizing the cards can be done in two ways:

- One card at a time as they are written
- After all the cards are written

Some indexers wait until all the cards are done. Then, on one card, they:

- Combine duplicate entries
- Eliminate synonymous entries
- List all page numbers for an entry in correct order

Other indexers prefer to put cards in alphabetical order as soon as they are written, which:

- Avoids duplication of cards
- Helps in the planning of a consistent arrangement
- Saves time in the final revision of the cards

In revising cards, watch for the following problems:

- Use consistent subject names. For example, both *atomic energy* and *nuclear energy* may have been used.
- Watch for singular and plural forms of the same word. For example, *mouse* and *mice*.
- Check for phrases that may be in more than one form, such as *inheritance of acquired characteristics* and *acquired characteristics, inheritance of*. If both forms are kept, be sure that the same page numbers are given in both places.
- Verify the cross-references to ensure that the items to which they refer have not been changed or eliminated.

Editing the cards

Once the cards are alphabetized, edit them by grouping headings, determining subheadings, and furnishing an adequate, but not excessive, number of cross-references.

From the headings and modifications on the cards, you now have to make final decisions about primary entries and subhead entries. Chose among synonymous or closely related terms and prepare suitable cross-references to reflect those choices.

Marking the cards for typing

After the cards have been arranged, they should be marked for typing. In a group of subentries under one heading, all main entries except the one on the first card should be crossed out, but not obliterated. If a subentry is followed by a secondary item, both main entry and subentry should be crossed out. See Figure 16.2 for examples of cards marked for typing.

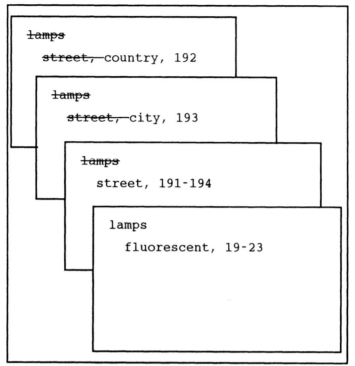

Figure 16.2 Marking the cards for typing

In a printed index, subentries are indented 1 em space, and secondary entries 2 em spaces. This is shown on the index cards by the marks □ and □□. The items in the cards listed in Figure 16.2 would be combined and marked for indentation as follows:

lamps
□fluorescent, 19–23
□street, 191–194
□□city, 193
□□country, 192

17

Automating the process

Doing it electronically

Indexing work is not recommended to those who lack an orderly mind and a capacity for taking pains. A good index is a minor work of art but it is also the product of clear thought and meticulous care.
— Peter Farrell, *How to Make Money From Home*

Objectives

In this chapter you will learn:
- What automating the indexing process means
- The types of automated indexing packages
- The process of entering information
- Where to place cross-references in electronic files
- About some cautions when automating the index process

What automating means

Automating the indexing process is really taking the index card model one step further. The computer helps speed up the process of entering headings and inversions, automatically alphabetizing the list, and then printing out the results.

Four automated methods

There are basically four types of automated indexing methods:

- Single-purpose indexing programs
- Electronic-publishing packages
- Word processors
- Indexing utilities

Single-purpose indexing programs

The single-purpose indexing program is designed only to create indexes. These packages usually are designed for intensive applications and are used by professional indexers to produce large and complex indexes.

These programs usually have built-in features that makes inverting headings easy. They also have strong alphabetizing capabilities that offer the user flexibility in choice. They allow the indexer to index to many levels. Additionally, single-purpose indexing programs permit flexibility in formatting the index and in laying out the index for final print.

These packages allow the creation of multiple indexes or combination of indexes into a master, or cumulative, index. (See Chapter 18 for more information about master indexes.)

Electronic-publishing packages

Most electronic-publishing software, or desktop-publishing software, incorporates indexing as a standard feature. The capabilities of the indexing feature vary.

These packages are getting highly sophisticated in their ability to create, format, and print out an index. They offer maximum control in entering terms, creating cross-references, permitting many levels of headings, offering flexible alphabetizing, allowing a variety of formats, and printing out the final index. Many of these packages are approaching, and some are surpassing, the capabilities of single-purpose indexing packages.

Word processors

More word processors are adding indexing features to their packages. These indexing programs are fairly sophisticated and permit the indexer to highlight words or type in words for entries. They also permit flexibility in layout and format. They do not usually allow much flexibility in alphabetizing choices. Many of these packages are approaching the capabilities of single-purpose and electronic publishing packages.

Indexing utilities

These programs are add-on features to existing packages, whether they be word processors or electronic publishing software. These utilities help streamline the tedious aspects of index marking by going through your document and marking words and phrases.

Basically, to use these programs you tell the utility the words and phrases you want indexed. The program then goes through your document and marks them. After going through your files and inserting the chosen index entries, you are free to return to your word processor or electronic publishing program to generate the index file and format it.

One indexing utility disparages the professional indexing community by implying that the program could index as well as a professional. "[This program] makes indexing so easy that you probably won't hire a professional indexer," says the reference guide.

Marking text is nothing more than a mechanical aspect of indexing. The true demands are in recognizing the appropriate passages to include, and that cannot be learned overnight, neither can it be turned over to an indexing utility. If a poor indexer uses an indexing utility, the result will be a quickly generated index, but a poor one.

The real strength in using indexing utilities is to use them to help the novice indexer by providing an easy way to mark everything in sight. Then the indexer can use the generated list to pick the more commonly used terms and to create entries for them.

Indexing utilities are not a replacement for a professional indexer.

Building an index electronically

Indexing electronically is basically the same as indexing with index cards. It involves marking text throughout the document, inputting that information into your program, generating the index file for that document, applying a style sheet or template to the generated index file, and then printing the file.

Marking text is done exactly as in manual indexing, as discussed in Chapter 16. You can mark as you go along or come back and do it all at once. You should enter cross-references as you mark your copy. You put the information into the program via the soft ware interface. Generating the index is accomplished by the program, usually with the indexer being able to determine various attributes of text and page number. Once the index is generated, the file is attached to a style sheet or template, which formats the index. Printing the index is also a function accomplished within the software package.

Additionally, you may be able to combine indexes into a master, or cumulative, index or create multiple indexes for the same book. (See Chapter 18 for more information about master indexes.)

After printing the index, edit it. To make corrections, you must return to the software package and edit the index entries. It is also possible to manually tweak the generated index file. If this is done, the changes will not be made to the original entries and, when the index is regenerated, the same corrections must be made again. It is best to edit the index entries. You should then test the index as you would an index created manually.

Electronic file placement

Here's a great tip on where to place your cross-references when using computer files. Place all *see* and *see also* references in one place—like at the end of the preface or Chapter 1. It is easier to find the terms this way if you need to edit them. If you scatter the cross-references throughout the files, you will have a difficult time locating the one you need to edit.

Some cautions

When evaluating any software for automating your indexing process, keep these considerations in mind:

1. Make sure that you can control the format of the index.
2. Be sure that you can control the methods of alphabetizing.
3. Make sure that you have the ability to control the final layout of the index.
4. Check for the ability to edit entries easily.
5. Make sure that the manual thoroughly explains the indexing process.
6. Don't believe the hype if your package says it can replace the indexer.
7. Until you know the package, always check the accuracy of the alphabetizing, cross-references, and locators.

Locating software

For a list of addresses of indexing software, see Appendix B, page 178.

18

Creating master indexes

Putting them all together

...the National Library of Medicine spends over $2 million and employs 44 full-time equivalent indexers just to index MEDLINE each year; simply as an economic proposition, therefore, human indexing might soon become a luxury for the makers of very large databases.
— Tom McFadden in "We Are What We Speak" in *ASI Newsletter*

Objectives

In this chapter you will learn:

- How to create master indexes
- When to use Roman numerals
- When to use abbreviated titles
- When to use Arabic numerals
- How to create useful footer designs

Master indexes

Master indexes are those indexes that span multiple volumes. These indexes include entries from all the documents in a particular document set. It takes some special planning on the part of the designer to produce effective master indexes. Particularly important is the structure of the book title, chapter, and page number.

The master index makes finding a particular subject easier across all volumes. The index can be located in several places in the document set:

- At the end of each physical volume
- As a separate document
- At the end of the last physical volume

Using Roman numerals

One method of identifying the volume for each would have you place a Roman numeral in the footer, which is the text that runs at the bottom of the page and indicates the page number and other information. Whichever method you use in the master index, you must identify the style at the beginning of the index, and maybe place reminders at the bottom of each page. Refer to page 194 for some sample notes.

Let's say you have a series of three diagnostic manuals as indicated below:

Diagnostics Documentation
   Processor Diagnostics (volume I)
   PBUS I/O System Diagnostics (volume II)
   Diagnostic Utilities (volume III)

To create an index entry for this example, precede each page number with a Roman numeral that indicates the volume referenced. Place a period between the volume number and the chapter, then a hyphen, then the page number:

command scripts, user-created   I.6-23, II.2-1, III.3-1

This entry indicates that references to user-created command scripts appear in volume I (*Processor Diagnostics*) on page 23 of Chapter 6, in volume II (*PBUS I/O System Diagnostics*) on page 1 of Chapter 2, and in volume III (*Diagnostic Utilities*) on page 1 of Chapter 3.

Using abbreviated titles

Another method is to create abbreviated titles instead of Roman numerals. For example:

Diagnostics Documentation
   Processor Diagnostics (pd)
   PBUS I/O System Diagnostics (io)
   Diagnostic Utilities (ut)

Using this method, you would have the following entry:

command scripts, user-created   pd.6-23, io.2-1, ut.3-1

Using Arabic numerals

Another method is to use Arabic numerals. For example:

Diagnostics Documentation
Processor Diagnostics (1)
PBUS I/O System Diagnostics (2)
Diagnostic Utilities (3)

Using this method, you would have the following entry:

command scripts, user-created   1.6-23, 2.2-1, 3.3-1

The locators can be difficult to spot quickly using Arabic numerals with a period. Using a slash (/) would help the reader spot the chapter number more quickly. For example:

command scripts, user-created   1/6-23, 2/2-1, 3/3-1

Footer designs

To make master indexes useful, ensure that footers, which are reflected in your page references in the index, contain all the information needed for your page references.

- The Roman numeral, abbreviated title, or Arabic numeral
- The chapter number
- The page number

Part Four
Completing
the Index

19

Formatting the index

Designing the layout

An index is a necessary implement, and no impediment, of a book except in the same sense wherein the carriages of an army are termed impediments. Without this, a large author is but a labyrinth, without a clue to direct the reader therein.
— Thomas Fuller, *Worthies of England*

Objectives

In this chapter you will learn:

- How to format your index
- The role typography plays in the index
- How to develop a style for your index

Formats and typography

Consider the following guidelines when you design the format of your index.

Basic page design

Indexes are usually set in two columns per page and in type that is two point sizes smaller than the size used in the text. This design works well if you took an average of between six and 10 references per page and if the desired length of the index is between 2 percent and 5 percent of the total pages of the book. If there are five or fewer references per book page, the index will be on the short end of this range; if there are more than 10 references per page, the index may be even more than 5 percent of the total book length.

Some indexes have three columns per page, and a very large book may have a four-column index. Multiple-column indexes are efficient space users, especially for indented indexes with their many short lines of headings and subheadings. If the index is set in more than two columns, the type size is usually dropped to three or four point sizes smaller than the book text.

Right-hand margins

Most indexes use a ragged-right style rather than a justified right margin. The problem with a justified right margin is that because of the narrow column widths, lines of type would frequently be crowded or widely spaced in order to come out justified.

Hyphenations

Most publishers do not allow word breaks because of the difficulty they may cause the reader. It you have to break a word, do it at the beginning or end of the word, not in the middle.

Index title

Give the index a title (usually *Index*). This can be centered or placed flush left. Simple linear design elements can be added, and the title can be emphasized by your choice of type size and style.

Letter headings

Leave extra white space between the different alphabetic sections of the index. You may want to place the appropriate capital letter or symbol in bold above each section.

Text attributes

Use style options like bold and italic to emphasize certain parts of the index. For example, you may:

- Put *see* references and *see also* references in italic
- Put page numbers for illustrations in italic
- Put page numbers for the primary treatment of a topic in bold

Tell the reader at the beginning of the index what conventions you are using in your index.

Create own chapter

Make the index a separate division of your document and format it in two or three columns.

Pagination

Paginate the index as if it were a continuation of the main text. Page numbers should follow the same style and be placed in the same position as in the main text.

Headers and footers

Create a running header or footer, or both, for the index. The header or footer should match the style and format of the header or footer in the main text.

Notational conventions

When indexing directory names, file names, keyboard key names, commands, and the like, use the same typeface and font as in the text. For example:

```
/hwdoc/lib/doc
CTRL
```

Entry formats

Index entry formats come two forms:

- Run-on, also called paragraph
- Line-by-line, also called indented

Run-on form

In a narrative work, the run-on form for entries is a good arrangement, because more often than not the sequence of the page numbers will correspond approximately to the sequence of the events recorded or to the time sequence in which the questions discussed were raised. The run-on format looks like this:

Dipole: characteristic impedance of, circular cross-section, 109; definition of, 55; effect of shape near drive point, 108; electric, 55, 66

Do not use the run-on format for indexes with more than two levels of headings because the entry becomes difficult, if not impossible, to decipher.

Line-by-line form

The run-on form is not efficient. The index is more efficient if the subheadings under any given main heading are printed on separate lines, arranged in alphabetical order. For example:

Dipole
    characteristic impedance of
       circular cross section, 109;
       multiwire cage, 113
       square cross section, 112
       triangular cross section, 112
    definition of, 55
    effect of shape near drive point, 108
    electric, 55, 66

In this example, the subheading "characteristic impedance of" is further split into four sub-subheadings. This is a fairly common practice, but avoid going beyond the third stage of subdivision.

Line wraps

Whenever a line of your index wraps, or continues to a second or third line, you must indent the line to separate it from lines of text preceding and following the line. A good standard indention is one em space longer than the maximum number of levels in your index. Notice the spacing following the main entry in the following example, which is a two-level index:

letter headings 35
letter-by-letter alphabetizing 69
   see also alphabetizing; word-by-word
       alphabetizing
   discussed 22, 67
   example 36

Jump entries

Entries that continue from one column to another in the index are called *jump entries*. When an entry jumps you must duplicate the levels of headings that precede the jumped entry. See Figure 19.1 for an example of a jump head.

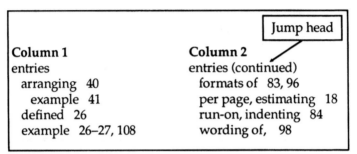

Figure 19.1   Example of a jump head

If you use a third-level jump entry, you must take the two preceding level headings with the third-level heading. See Figure 19.2 for an example of multiple-level jump heads.

Figure 19.2   Example of multiple-level jump heads

Indention

All indexes are set with hanging indention. That is, the first line of each complete entry is flush left, while all other lines of the entry are indented to some degree. Hanging indention is used because alphabetical listings are more readily scanned when the key word is thus set off.

With run-on (paragraph) indexes, indention decisions are simple: the main entry begins flush left, and all run-over lines in that entry are indented the same degree. With an indented index, however, there may be several levels of indention, each indicating a specific relationship between the parts of the entry.

The usual measure of indention is one em space, which is the horizontal space the capital "M" takes for the type size of the index. For a line-by-line (indented) index, the main entry is flush left. Run-over lines for all entries—main entries as well as subentries—are indented to the same degree, which is usually one em-space more than the longest subheading indention. For example, if you have three levels of indention, the run-over lines will be indented four em spaces.

Figure 19.3 has three levels of indention. Note that run-over lines are indented four em spaces.

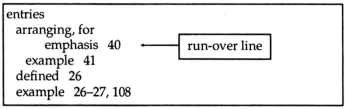

```
entries
   arranging, for
         emphasis  40         run-over line
   example  41
   defined  26
   example  26–27, 108
```

Figure 19.3 Sample indents

Details of style

It is important to decide on an indexing style before putting index entries in your document. Find out if your department or company already has an indexing style guide. If there is an indexing style guide, stick to it. If there is not an indexing style guide, see Appendix E on page 197 for a sample one that may be used as the basis for creating your own.

The indexing style guide contains a summary of why to index, as well as what to index and what not to index. Other standards described include how to:

- Create entries and subentries
- Use cross-references
- Format the index
- Break columns
- Separate entries and subentries
- Punctuate the index
- Sort the index
- Edit and verify the index
- Create master indexes

When preparing the index, follow these details of the style:

- Initial words may be uppercase or lowercase—just be consistent.
- Run-on lines of entries of more than one line are indented the depth of one em space.
- A colon or an em space follows a topic when it is modified.
- A comma or an em space follows a topic when it is not modified.
- Commas separate page numbers within an entry or subentry.
- A period precedes a *see* cross-reference.
- Semicolons separate two or more entries in cross-references.
- There is no end punctuation.
- Parentheses may be used to differentiate homonyms, which are people or things with identical names, for example:

  screen (computer)
  screen (to cover)

- Avoid going beyond the third level of entries.

20

Managing the index

Calculating size, time, and cost

The most accomplished way of using books at present is twofold: either, first, to serve them as men do lords,—learn their titles exactly and then brag of their acquaintance; or, secondly, which is, indeed, the choicer, the profounder, and politer method, to get a thorough insight into the index, by which the whole book is governed and turned, like fishes by the tail.
— Jonathan Swift, *A Tale of A Tub*

Objectives
In this chapter you will learn how to:
- Determine the size of an index
- Calculate the cost and time for indexing

Determining the size

While the size of an index is no indication of quality, a short index in a long document should make you suspicious. The minimum size for an index can be calculated in several ways.

- One entry for every 100 words of text
- One double-column page (type size is $^{10}/12$ on an 18-pica wide line by 56 picas deep) of index entries for every 20 pages of text, not including:
  - Flow charts
  - Front matter
  - Lists of operation codes, abbreviations, program labels, and messages
  - Figures, examples, tables, and blank pages longer than three-quarters of a page

  For example, a typical 200-page manual, with 50 pages of figures, examples, etc., should have an index about seven double-column pages long.

- For the average book of 282 pages, there are 1,045 lines of index developed (about eight pages of three-column text in 8-point type on 9-point leading).
- The typical index contains 3.7 lines per page indexed.

Calculating time and cost

You cannot create an index overnight. No adequate index for a manual of any complexity can be—or should be—completed over a weekend. Indexing requires intense intellectual concentration.

Good indexing requires reflection, and reflection demands time. You must have the time to stop frequently, review a bit of the job just completed, try putting yourself in the place of the technical writer on one hand and the reader on the other, and decide whether both have been served by the decisions you have made.

Estimating time

Because indexing is quite a complex activity, it takes more time than many technical writers imagine. Creating an index is no different than creating a typical chapter of text.

An experienced indexer needs between 30 and 44 hours to create the index for a 220-page manual:

3 hours	Preliminary rapid reading of text
10 hours	Reading text and marking passages online for index entries (add 14 more hours if this part is done on hard copy)
8 hours	Inputting entries in publishing system
7 hours	Editing index and inputting corrections
2 hours	Generating and printing index
30–44 hours	

An inexperienced indexer needs between 55 and 83 hours to create that same index for a 220-page manual:

3 hours	Preliminary rapid reading of text
20 hours	Reading text and marking passages online for index entries (add 28 more hours if this part is done on hard copy)
16 hours	Inputting entries in publishing system
14 hours	Editing index and inputting corrections
2 hours	Generating and printing index
55–83 hours	

The addition of 14 to 28 hours for marking text on hard copy is the time it takes to convert from the cards or hard copy markups to inputting the index entries in the computer program. It is much quicker to index online!

Estimating cost

It is easiest to calculate the cost for creating and editing an index by the number of pages in the manual. The per-page system is the best way to determine how much time the indexer will spend on a project. This method is also used often because every page of text has to be read and evaluated for indexable items. Typical per-page rates are $3–$5 per page, depending on geographic location, degree of technical difficulty, and denseness of the text. Using the rates above, the index for a 200-page manual would cost somewhere between $400 and $800 to produce.

Real-world examples

It would be a good investment to keep your management numbers in a spreadsheet so you can see what you are doing on an ongoing basis.

Figures 20.1 through 20.6 contain examples of one such spreadsheet showing critical data on all elements of managing an index.

In this example, the average book was 288 pages and was in-house for 16 days. It took 36.9 hours over 10.3 days to complete the index.

The 36.9 hours were spent as follows:

18.4 hours =	.4	Review	CREATE
	2.3	Markup	
	15.7	Input	
8.1 hours =	4.5	Edit	EDIT
	3.6	Input edit	
10.5 hours =	5.4	Administrative	ADMIN
	5.1	Eat 'em	

Tracking time to index

Figure 20.1 shows how to track jobs coming in, turnaround times, and days indexing.

A	B	C	D	E	F	G	H	I
Date information	1	2	3	4	5	6		Averages
Title of book	SCO Muti	Novell	Ad	SOL	SCO Client	USDA		
Number of pages	420	406	78	394	376	54		288 0
Date received	3/17/92	4/8/92	5/8/92	5/6/92	5/26/92	9/1/92		
Date due	4/14/92	4/28/92	5/12/92	5/27/92	6/9/92	9/18/92		
Date returned	4/13/92	5/4/92	5/11/92	5/13/92	6/8/92	9/16/92		
Days early or late	1	-6	1	9	1	0		-2
Days in house	27	26	3	12	13	15		16 0
Start indexing date	3/27/92	4/20/92	5/8/92	5/12/92	5/27/92	9/1/92		
End indexing date	4/13/92	5/3/92	5/9/92	5/17/92	6/7/92	9/16/92		
Days indexing	17	13	1	5	11	15		10 3

Figure 20.1 Example of tracking time to index

Tracking hours to create

Figure 20.2 shows how to track preliminary review of a document, marking up the text, and inputting entries.

Hours indexing								
Preliminary review	1 0	0 3	0 8	0 8	0 2	0 8		0 4
% total time	1 2%	0 5%	10%	2 3%	0 5%	2 0%		0 8%
Marking up text	3 0	3 2	1 6	3 5	2 7	0 8		2 3
% total time	3 6%	7 3%	11 1%	9 9%	6 6%	2 0%		6 5%
Inputting entries	25 4	20 .	5 3	21 3	17 0	4 8		15 7
% total time	30 8%	49 8%	36 4%	60 7%	42 1%	56 1%		46 0%
TOTAL CREATE TIME	29 4	23 5	6 9	25 6	20 2	4 6		18 4
TOTAL CREATE %	35 7%	58 3%	47 5%	72 9%	49 1%	56 1%		53 3%

Figure 20.2 Example of tracking hours to create an index

Tracking editing time

Figure 20.3 shows how to track edit time and input edits.

Editing time	171	31	0 3	1 0	2 9	2 5	4 5
% total time	20 3%	7 7%	0 3%	2 9%	7 1%	30 5%	11 8%
Edr input time	3 0	7 2	1 2	1 6	7 9	0 5	3 6
% total time	3 6%	17 9%	7 9%	4 6%	19 2%	6 1%	9 9%
TOTAL EDIT TIME	20 1	10 3	1 5	2 6	10 8	3 0	8 0
TOTAL EDIT %	24 4%	25 5%	10 2%	7 4%	26 3%	36 6%	21 7%

Figure 20.3 Example of tracking editing time

Tracking administrative time

It's important to keep track of administrative time, which includes time on the phone to clients, eliminating software problems, doing parts of a job over because you didn't adhere to style standards, and the like. Figure 20.4 shows how to track administrative time.

Administrative time	6 1	6 4	4 3	5 6	9 6	0 6	5 4
% total time	7 4%	15 9%	29 6%	16 0%	23 4%	7 1%	16 6%
Eat 'em time	26 9	0	9	3	0 5	0 0	5 1
% total time	32 6%	0 2%	12 8%	3 7%	1 2%	0 0%	8 4%
TOTAL ADMIN TIME	33 0	6 5	6 2	6 9	10 1	0 6	10 5
TOTAL ADMIN %	40 0%	16 1%	42 4%	19 7%	24 6%	7 1%	25 0%
Total time indexing	82 4	40 3	14 6	35 1	41 1	8 2	36 9

Figure 20.4 Example of tracking administrative time

Tracking statistics

The key to knowing what to charge, how long to complete an index, and how thoroughly a job you do can be tracked also. Some vital statistics include number of entries, number of cross-references, rate per page, rate per entry, rate per hour, pages per hour, entries per page, and entries per hour. Figure 20.5 shows how to track certain statistics.

Statistics							
Number of entries	1,479	2,275	895	2,465	1,675	476	1,545
Number of characters				79,533			79,533
Number of words				15,907			15,907
Number of sees	48	4	0	50	63	3	28
Number of see alsos	8	73	0	0	43	18	24
Total number cross-refs	56	77	0	50	106	21	52
Rate per page	$3	$3	$6	13	$3		$3.60
Rate per entry	$0.85	$0.54	$0.52	$0.48	$0.67		$0.61
Rate per hour	$15.29	$30.20	$32.10	$33.70	$27.45		$27.75
Pages per hour	8.5	12.0	9.3	14.0	12.1	7.1	10.5
Entries per page	15	56	115	63	45	88	67
Entries per hour	29.9	67.2	106.5	87.5	54.2	62.6	68.0
Amount billed	$1,260.00	$1,218.00	$468.00	$1,182.00	$1,128.00		$1,051.20

Figure 20.5 Example of tracking statistics

Tracking account information

Of course, it's important to keep track of your moneys, invoices, days invoices outstanding, overhead, expenditures, and salary. The bottom line is profit or loss. Figure 20.6 shows how to track accounting information.

Accounting							
P.O. number	517920785	517921117	3867	517921373	517921525		
Invoice number	041492018	051892028	051192018	051892018	061192018		
Invoice date	4/14/92	5/18/92	5/11/92	5/18/92	6/11/92		
Payment received	5/26/92	6/29/92	5/26/92	6/29/92	7/27/92		
Days outstanding	42	42	15	42	46		37.4
Expenditures	$60.01	$27.24	$8.40	$36.14	$31.05	$7.98	$28.47
Overhead	$130.00	$130.00	$130.00	$130.00	$130.00	$130.00	$130.00
Salary	$1,069.00	$800.00	$290.00	$780.00	$752.00		
Profit or loss	$9.99	$260.76	$39.60	$315.86	$214.95		$444.32

Figure 20.6 Example of tracking accounting information

Charting the issues

It's much easier to see the information charted. Figures 20.7 through 20.10 contain charts of a few measurements.

Charting total time

Figure 20.7 shows how long it took to create the index, edit the index, and administer the index.

Total time

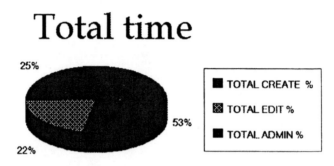

Figure 20.7   Example of charting total time

Charting creation time

Figure 20.8 shows how long it took to do preliminary reviews, marking up text, and inputting entries.

Creation time

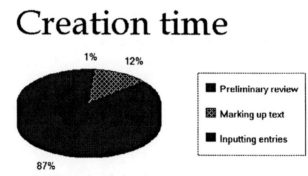
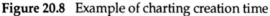

Figure 20.8   Example of charting creation time

Charting editing time

Figure 20.9 shows how long it takes to edit an index and input edits.

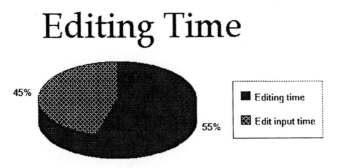

Figure 20.9   Example of charting editing time

Charting administrative time

Figure 20.10 shows how long it takes to administrate the entire indexing job.

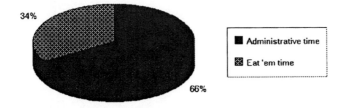

Figure 20.10 Example of charting administrative time

21

Editing the index

A helpful checklist

The most common refrain was that software
documentation is poorly indexed, and as a result you can't
find the answers you need.
— Christine Grech in "Computer Documentation Doesn't
Pass Muster" in *PC/Computing*

Objectives
In this chapter you will learn how to:
- Edit the index
- Check index format
- Locate *see* and *see also* notices
- How to edit line-by-line indexes
- How to edit run-on indexes
- How to use an editing checklist

Always edit the index

Marking the text and entering the entries are just the beginning of the indexing process. During the drafting of the index, you are most concerned with creating individual entries and their subentries. During editing, concern shifts to the index as a cohesive, accurate, consistent work.

Just as when you edit your manual, editing the index may require:

- Creating or deleting entries
- Splitting or combining entries
- Regrouping or rewording entries
- Verifying entries to make them error-free
- Ensuring the order and consistency of entries

Index format

The format and arrangement of the index are important. The general sequence is:

- Symbols and special characters
- Alphabetic subjects
- Numeric subjects

In formatting the index, make the first line of the entry a hanging indent. Indent secondary entries one em space. Indent tertiary entries two em spaces. For example:

primary entry
  secondary entry
    tertiary entry

It is also important to watch for entries that wrap to another line. The line that wraps should be indented one em space deeper than the last level of subheading. For example:

population configuration map, abbreviate
  PCM 176, 354

See and *see also* locations

A *see* reference immediately follows the main entry. Generally, a *see also* reference is located as the first or last secondary or tertiary entry. Entries with only one subheading should be on one line.

Line-by-line indexes

In line-by-line formats, the primary entry is followed by secondary and tertiary entries. The locator is preceded by either a comma or an em space. For example:

dipole
  see also magnetism
  characteristic impedance of
    circular cross-section, 109
    multiwire cage, 113
    square cross-section, 112
    triangular cross-section, 112
  definition of, 55
  effect of shape near drive point, 108
  electric, 55, 66

Or do it this way:

dipole
  see also magnetism
  characteristic impedance of
    circular cross-section   109
    multiwire cage   113
    square cross-section   112
    triangular cross-section   112
  definition of   55
  effect of shape near drive point   108
  electric   55, 66

Run-on indexes

In the run-on format, the topic is entered followed by a colon, then the subheadings, then the locator. A semicolon separates secondary headings. For example:

> dipole: characteristic impedance of, circular
> cross-section, 109; definition of, 55; effect of
> shape near drive point, 108; electric, 55, 66.
> *See also* magnetism

Editing checklist

To ensure an accurate and complete index, use the following checklist to verify the specific items in the index.

☐ Check the alphabetic sequence throughout each edit pass and particularly at final edit. Check primary entries for strict alphabetical order.

☐ Check the levels of subentries so that the proper indentation shows the relationship of each entry to the preceding one.

☐ Check the subjects to determine whether slight variations of wording are intentional or whether only one wording should be used.

☐ Check the subjects for duplication due to differences in capitalizing.

☐ Check the number of page references following a subject. If there are more than four, consider creating more specific subentries.

☐ As part of the check for completeness and accuracy, be sure to check each occurrence of a topic to see that the page references are the same and that they appear in every occurrence.

☐ Check each subentry to determine whether it should also appear as a primary entry.

☐ Check to determine whether the subentries should be rearranged to stress a certain point.

- ☐ Check the number of subentries under the various forms of the same topic to see that they are the same.

- ☐ Check each *see* reference to verify that it refers to an entry that is followed by subentries with the proper page references.

- ☐ Check the wording of the subjects in *see* and *see also* references.

- ☐ Check text references to verify that they still exist in the index in the same form as in the text reference.

- ☐ Check cross-references to make sure they go somewhere and that headings are identical. Make sure the cross-references are needed; if only a few page references are involved, add these to the original heading and delete the cross-reference. Also make sure their placement within the entries is consistent.

- ☐ Check the reasonableness of page numbers (no "12122" or "193–93"), and make sure that sequences of page references are in ascending order.

- ☐ Check subentries for consistency of order, whether alphabetical, chronological, or other. If *mentioned* or some other such device is used, make sure that the use is consistent.

- ☐ If some entries seem overanalyzed (many subentries with only one page reference each), try to combine some of them. If subheadings are longer and more elaborate than necessary, try to simplify them.

- ☐ Check whether references to place names or personal names that are used only as examples are indexed or omitted consistently. While many indexers do not index them, they aid in completeness.

- ☐ Check that there is at least one index entry for every table, illustration, diagram, photograph, figure, graphic, chart, map, or other visual aid.

- ☐ Check that any notational conventions in the text, such as monospace, key cap font, or italic, are also applied to index entries.

☐ Make sure that jump entries—those that continue on another column— have the proper headings carried over to that column top.

☐ Check to see that wrap lines (lines of an entry that are longer than one line) are indented at least one em space longer than the number of levels of subheadings used in the index.

Sample edited index

Refer to page 193 for a sample of an edited index.

22

Testing the index

Usability aids

The chief purpose of an index is distillation, and in
performing that task it can manage to suggest a life's
incongruities with a concision that the most powerful
biographical stylist will have trouble matching.
— Thomas Mallon in "The Best Part of Every Book Comes
Last" in *The New York Times*

Objectives
In this chapter you will learn:
- Methods of conducting usability tests on indexes
- How to perform six usability tests

Testing the five basic criteria

This section discusses ways to test the five basic criteria for a good index. A good index:

- Is accurate
- Has appropriate depth
- Is concise
- Is cross-referenced
- Is logical

Accuracy

Test for accuracy, first, by spot checking a few pages. Choose two or three entries in each column and look up all the page references given. Is the subject listed in the index covered on the pages cited? If the index fails this first test of accuracy, all other tests become unnecessary.

Verify the alphabetical order, even in computer-generated index. This sounds like an easy task, but alphabetizing is a surprisingly complex process. Use either word-by-word or letter-by-letter alphabetizing, but usage must be consistent within a single index.

Ask these questions to determine how accurate your index is:

- Are the terms used correctly in the index?
- Are the spelling, capitalizing, italicizing, and punctuation used in the book followed?
- Is the alphabetizing accurate, whether word-by-word or letter-by-letter?
- Check a sample of references to be sure the material indexed is actually on the page cited.

Accuracy in the choice of index terms may be tested by checking some technical and some ambiguous terms in the index against the passages they refer to in order to make sure the terms chosen are appropriate.

Appropriate depth

You can assess depth by taking a few sample pages of text, identifying the important topics covered, and looking up the topics in the index to make sure they are included. This test will also reveal how well you have used headings and subheadings to organize the material.

Ask yourself these questions to determine if your index has the depth needed for your user:

- Are all important topics (concepts, subjects, proper names, and so on) and pertinent statements represented in the index? Check several.
- Are entries sufficiently specific to permit ready access to the desired material yet sufficiently comprehensive to prevent scattering of related terms? Headings chosen should be concise, each referring to one particular subject.
- Are there adequate cross-references to guide the user to main entries or other entries offering additional information?
- Are there duplicate entries instead of cross-references where space permits?

Test the index for depth in two ways:

1. Choose a few passages from the work and check the index for the terms representing the major topics discussed. If the index fails to locate the selected passages through the terms chosen in more than 5 percent of the attempts, something is wrong.

   In that case, a further test should be made: Attempt to locate the selected passages through more general or broader terms than those originally chosen. If this succeeds, then the terms in the index are not sufficiently specific.

2. Scan the index for terms having a noticeably large number of page references. Good indexers try to give no more than 10–12 references for any one term, avoiding strings of page numbers.

Conciseness

The purpose of conciseness is to eliminate scattering.
Scattering occurs when information of like ideas is spread
among diverse headings and various synonyms. Two
points help to remedy this problem:

- Analyze your audience and find out which term is the
single most appropriate pointer term. Look in
competitors' manuals to see which single terms
appear most often in their indexes.

- Put *see also* references beneath words to direct the
reader to synonyms that point to closely related
information.

Cross-references

Another way to ensure that cross-references are used
correctly is to list the same topics in two or more places.
For example, you might list *stereo radio* in two places: once
as *stereo radio* and once as *radio, stereo*.

You should take the time to verify that the *see* and *see also*
headings are exactly the same as the actual entries.
Nothing is more maddening to the user than a
cross-reference loop that leads the reader on a winding
path. No index should tell a reader who looks up *memory*
to see *random access memory*, which then sends the reader to
see *computer memory*.

Even worse, never refer the reader to a *blind entry*, that is,
an entry that doesn't exist! That's the mortal sin of
indexing.

Only necessary cross-references should be included. For a
subject entry with no subheadings, it takes less space to
insert the page references under two different headings (for
example, *users* and *consumers*) than it does to lead the
reader unnecessarily from one to the other with a *see*
reference.

A *see also* reference must lead to additional information, not to the same page references under a second heading. Accurate, logical, and useful cross-references are the hallmarks of a good index.

Logicalness

You can assess whether an index has logical topics by asking yourself these questions:

- Is the entry appropriate to the material indexed?
- Does it permit easy and quick scanning and ready pinpointing of the desired references?
- Are the main entries easily differentiated from subentries?
- Is the arrangement of subentries readily apparent?
- Do subentries bear a logical and grammatical relationship to main entries?
- If any explanations are required, are they easily spotted and lucid?
- When a reference covers several consecutive pages, are the beginning and the end of the reference indicated clearly?
- Do page references differentiate between principal discussion and cursory mention of the topic?
- If there are deviations from the normal alphabetical order, or if some other order (such as chronological) is employed, is this necessary and is it obvious to the user?
- Are terms used consistently in the index?
- Is a topic that is indexed by a specific term in one passage indexed by the same term (not a broader or narrower one) in another passage? (If a recipe on lamb stew is indexed in a cookbook under *lamb*, then a recipe on leg of lamb must also be indexed under *lamb*, not under *meat*.

Some other usability tests

Usability testing is a method to test the effectiveness of your index. The best way to make sure your index is as good as it can be is for you to study the best indexes in your field and see how they are structured. Then make sure your indexes follow that structure.

No matter what the book, the index should be examined and tested. Tests such as those listed below will soon rub in the requirements of a good index, and the types of references that are needed. Try some of these methods to determine if your index is complete and useful.

Paragraph picking

A good way of testing is to read a paragraph and then to try to discover the topics it has been indexed under. If it is easy to discover the topics, then the index is good; if they are difficult to discover, then the index is poor.

Boldface page numbers

Check to see if main page references, illustrations, tables, or the like, are indicated in the index. For example, if you have several page references to a given topic, indicate which is the main page reference by putting that page number in bold type:

> stereo radio   3, **10**, 19, 50

Spot checking entries, subjects

The exhaustiveness of an index can be a quick predictor of the quality of a manual. One index test is to:

- Choose one or two items from each alphabetic section of the index and look them up in the document.
- Then choose one or two items from selected pages and look them up in the index.

If the index fails to help you find items easily, or if the index is incomplete, it is unsatisfactory. This simple test can serve as a strong indicator of the quality of other portions of the manual that are not so apparent.

Checking completeness

To check the completeness of both your index and text, compare your index to a competitor's index. If the competitor has an index word or term you don't, check to see whether it is because you haven't included the word in the index or if your manual has left out that information.

23

Indexing tips

Some final thoughts

I cannot believe that I am the only person in the world who
finds it necessary to be perpetually leaping up from the
meal-table to exact some apposite reference from his
library. Fellow-leapers will know only too well that half an
index is often worse than no index at all, and that
inadequacy in this department results in one's return,
empty-handed, to an anapolaustic table of wrath.
— Rodney Dale, *The Tumour in the Whale: A Collection of
Modern Myths*

Objectives

In this chapter you will learn:
- Five tips for better indexing
- What things not to index
- Some do's and don'ts

Twelve tips for better indexing

Here are 12 tips to make indexing an easier and more accurate experience:

- Always index in the same manner. Develop a habit of indexing while writing.
- Place index terms at the word or phrase to be indexed when indexing online.
- At a minimum, create one reference to each table and figure. You are encouraged to include several references for each table and figure. Tables and figures often contain large amounts of detailed and varied information. By having access to several different references, readers are more likely to find the information they need.
- Generate the index frequently and keep it handy to check spellings, plurals, and so on.
- Be consistent.
- Integrate indexing into the documentation process.
- Schedule it in your documentation plan.
- Start indexing early; don't let it go until the end.
- Review the index with the rest of the documentation.
- Give copies of the document and draft index to beta testers and product support.
- Give copies to other writers to check for accuracy, appropriate depth, conciseness, cross-referencing, and logicalness.
- Always have the index edited by an editor.

Things not to be indexed

Here are some things that are not normally indexed:

- Authors and titles listed in the bibliography and cited as references
- Unimportant mentions of subjects in discursive notes
- Names of people mentioned in prefatory matter, such as acknowledgments and revision histories
- Information on the title page

Some do's and don'ts

Here are a few of the things you *should* do when indexing:

- Do take plenty of time for the initial planning—mistakes made here will never be retrieved.
- Do be accurate. Never guess or rely on being virtually certain—check it out.
- Do check up on all queries before you put the cards or entries into alphabetical order.
- Do train your memory.

Here are some things you should *not* do when indexing:

- Do not enter different references to the same person, place, thing, event, or topic under different topics.
- Do not make references to similar things or topics under one topic.
- Do not overindex the first 50 pages.
- Do not, for convenience in editing, skimp on descriptions and modifications. This will help you prune the index at the very last to the required length.

Part Five
Considering
the Future

24

Online indexing

Point the way

The solution to inaccessible documentation can be as simple and low-tech as making a better index....With proper indexing, ten percent more effort will double the accessibility of information. Moreover, most of your efforts to improve the indexing of online documents will improve paper documents as well.
— William Horton, "A quick (and not too dirty) fix for online documentation," in *Technical Communication*

Objectives

In this chapter you will learn:
- Criteria for a good online index
- How to create search strategies
- Pros and cons of online indexes

Human vs. machine indexing

For documentation—online or hard copy—to be successful, access is the essential ingredient for the document's usability. A good index makes access easier, and that is the main purpose of the index. And indexing for online documents is exactly the same as for hard copy!

To create the best indexes, it must be done manually, not generated by a computer or through full-text search. Some reasons that humans should generate the index rather than using tool-based indexing include:

- An index is an intellectual analysis process, one that computers have yet to master even primitively.
- Because the body text contains the answers to a user's questions and not the question itself, a human can anticipate the wording necessary when indexing by the answer-the-question method. Even if the automated system can infer the meaning from the words present, it lacks the subtlety to express this meaning in terms that a naive user will employ when searching for that information.
- Tool-based indexing requires a controlled vocabulary aid, like a thesaurus, so terms are the same, and only people can decide which terms to keep, remove, and put under broader or narrower terms, which is particularly useful in team indexing or to maintain consistency.
- While computers as expert systems can be valuable, they cannot be substituted for human intervention for things like spell checking, using proper word order, maintaining the index, and phrase permutations, like inverting terms.
- Research shows that two people match less than 50 percent of the time when analyzing the same passage, and some deduce from that that human-authored terms will fail more often than they succeed. But, most retrieval tests show that most computer-authored terms do not match 50 percent of the time either.

- Technical documents, by their nature, contain uncommon words and phrases that makes recognition by automated systems difficult.
- Conceptual indexes provide direct access to significant ideas from any point in a document, not just the names of things that can be found easily by search features.
- Much of the information in technical documents is graphical, such as tables, syntax diagrams, and screen images, which most automated systems cannot peer into and make sense of, nor are the short labels and captions of much help to the automated system.

Hypertext defined

Hypertext is an extension of the text or document. It is a way of moving about a document via hyperspace, which is a geometry with many dimensions. Hypertext is a multidimensional text. One dimension is the internal structure. Another dimension is the relationships among the text. Still another dimension is the ability of people to communicate as they manipulate text.

There are four types of text in hypertext:
- Text, which is one document
- Microtext, which is a piece of one document
- Macrotext, which is many documents
- Grouptext, which is where text is shared so people can communicate directly.

There are three way to access hypertext documents:
- Reading, which implies the traditional, sequential, line-by-line approach from page one to the end
- Browsing, which involves jumping from place to place and only reading small segments in each of those places
- Searching, which occurs when a person knows the name for some information and wants only that specific information

Growing interest

There is a growing interest in using hypertext for indexing purposes. This interest is based on:

- Increased availability of online electronic material
- Recognition of benefits arising from the union of hypertext and indexing
- Software manufacturers adding hypertext capabilities to their new products.

Studies show that reading from paper is faster than reading from computer screens by a factor of 30 percent. In some instances, such as when there is confusion over page-turning commands or there are anxieties that some users have in reading from a computer, then the time to read a text on a computer screen doubles. Yet, online documentation is becoming a reality because of costs and because the graphical user interfaces and software make it easier to use.

Criteria for a good online index

A good online index meets the following criteria:

- Provides multiple entry points
- Includes consistent access routes
- Follows users ideas
- Is very detailed
- Ensures quick access to information
- Is easy to read

The most important criteria is providing multiple entry points so that there are many different terms that point to the same information. By this definition, a good index is one where all the guesses of the reader seem to find an entry point in the index.

A good online index also provides consistent access routes. This is easily accomplished by making sure that you use inverted terms. For example, if you use

commas
    with telephone numbers, 234

then be sure to invert the headings to ensure consistent access routes:

telephone numbers
    commas with, 234

Or place a *see also* cross-reference at the entry:

telephone numbers
    see also commas

Searching strategies

Users bring their own world of experience and expertise into play when using an index. Because of this, users will approach an index differently. Some will peruse the word listings and let the list prompt them. Some will look up a related item and go to that section. Some try to use the typographical cues given. Some lose track of where they are when carrying out a search.

Because there is so much difference in strategy, it is important to make your index as complete as possible. Most index users can think of only three or four alternative words or categories as entry points to words they find. To make search strategies work for online indexes, always keep in mind that it is the user's background knowledge on any given subject that determines how the search will be done.

25

Indexing standards

For whom the norm tolls

... a good index provides readers with the scope and content of the entire book in a highly condensed overview, as though the author's outline and treatment were shuffled and reassembled in alphabetical order.
— June Morse in "How to Recognize a Good Index" in *The Editorial Eye*

Objectives
In this chapter you will learn:
- About the necessity of standards
- Organizations that create standards
- About different types of indexing standards
- What generic markup is

Necessity of standards

A *standard* is something that is considered to be a model to be used as a basis of comparison. While indexing is a creative activity, the process itself defies standardization. If the same text is indexed by different indexers, the results will be slightly or even substantially different. Even when the same text is indexed a second or third time by the same indexer, the resulting indexes will vary.

However, the technical details of indexing do lend themselves to standardization. Since the 1950s, several national and international organizations have been developing indexing standards. These groups have tried to create standards on the construction of indexes from alphabetizing to indexing terminology, to achieve consistency without compromising the innate dynamic nature of indexing.

A bad index or the lack of an index are the major complaints about technical documents. Why are there so many bad indexes? Many of the causes can be found in an ignorance of or neglecting to use the good indexing practices recommended by indexing standards. Adherence to standards promotes fewer flawed and outright bad indexes. While standards are never perfect, they generally contain the best available guidance for novice as well as experienced indexers.

Standards organizations

The National Information Standards Organization (NISO) in the United States and the British Standards Institution (BSI) in the United Kingdom are the two organizations that are instrumental in producing indexing standards

The British standard, BS 3700, is titled *British Standard Recommendations for Preparing Indexes to Books, Periodicals and Other Documents* and was released in 1988.

The U.S. standard, ANSI/NISO Z39.4, is titled *American National Standard Guidelines for Indexes for Information Retrieval*, and a new version was scheduled for release in 1993.

BSI is an independent national body that issues standards in virtually all fields and on several thousands of technical, scientific, and intellectual subjects.

NISO, on the other hand, is more specialized. It develops national standards on indexing and related topics and is concerned primarily with standards concerned with information, library work, and publishing. NISO succeeded Committee Z39 of the American National Standards Institute (ANSI), with which NISO is now affiliated as an independent body. All standards issued by NISO are authorized as American National Standards by ANSI.

The International Organization for Standardization (ISO), which has about 70 national standardizing bodies including BSI and NISO, develops standards on information, among them several on indexing and related topics. In 1982 ISO issued their indexing standards in *Information Transfer*.

ANSI/NISO Z39.4

This standard provides guidelines for the content, organization, and presentation of indexes used for the retrieval of documents and parts of documents. But it does not attempt to set standards for every detail or technique of indexing. These can be determined for each index on the basis of type of material being indexed, medium of the index, method of presentation for searching, and the user for whom the index is designed.

Z39.4 deals with the principles of indexing, regardless of type of material being indexed, the method of index, the medium of the index, or the method of presentation searching. This standard concerns itself with both online indexing as well as traditional back-of-the-book indexing.

It also includes:
- Definitions of indexes and their parts
- Treatment of the nature and variety of indexes
- Recommendations about the design, organization, and presentation of indexes

Generic markup

More and more indexers now submit an electronic manuscript, which is an ASCII text file that can be moved easily from one computer to another, because the ASCII characters have been standardized (ISO 646).

ASCII is a coding scheme that assigns a specific numeral value to each character. *Generic markup* is the process of assigning groups of ASCII characters to label parts of an electronic manuscript, for example, headings, words in italic, sections (such as an index), and special characters not defined by ASCII.

As more and more indexers submit electronic manuscripts by modem and diskette, the federal government, major publishers, and software houses have funded efforts to develop and apply generic markup techniques.

There are two markup styles in widespread use. One was developed by the Association of American Publishers and later became ANSI/NISO Z39.59, *Electronic Manuscripts: Preparation and Markup*; the other is the *Chicago Guide to Preparing Electronic Manuscripts for Authors and Publishers* (1987). ANSI/NISO Z39.59 is a fully complying application of the Standard Generalized Markup Language (SGML).

One document, *Generic Markup of Electronic Index Manuscripts*, presents both markup styles. For example, Figure 25.1 is the printed result of text file coding according to ANSI/NISO Z39.59 (see Figure 25.2) and Chicago (see Figure 25.3).

```
indexers
  free-lance, 21, 44
  standards for, 242–244
  see also publishers

publishers
  John Wiley, 15
  McGraw-Hill, 12–13
```

Figure 25.1 Printed manuscript based on generic
markups

```
<itm>indexers
<sit2>free-lance, <b>21</b>, 44
<sit2>standards for, 242&ndash;244
<sit2><it>see also</it>publishers
<itm>publishers
<sit2>John Wiley, <it>15</it>
<sit2>McGraw-Hill, 12&ndash;13
```

Figure 25.2 Text file coded according to ANSI/NISO
Z39.59

```
<x1>indexers</xi>
<x2>free-lance, <el>21</el>, 44</x2>
<x2>standards for, 242<n>244</x2>
<x2><i>see also</i>publishers</x2>
<sp>
<x1>publishers</x1>
<x2>John Wiley, <i>15</i>
<x2>McGraw-Hill, 12<n>13</x2>
```

Figure 25.3 Text file coded according to Chicago

Part Six
Additional
Information

A

Bibliography

For more information

Develop an index, based on key words or concepts, for
user documents over eight pages.
— *IEEE Standard for Software User Documentation*, IEEE Std
1063-1987

Overview

This bibliography contains a list of books and journal
articles on indexes and indexing.

Altman, Rick. "Indexing software for Ventura Publisher," *Computer Currents* (Fort Worth-Dallas), 1991, 3(9):12.

American Society of Indexers. "Specifications for printed indexes," *The Indexer*, 1974, 9(3):121–122.

Anderson, Paul V. "Provide an index if it is useful," in *Technical Writing: A Reader-Centered Approach.* San Diego: Harcourt Brace Jovanovich. 1987. pp. 318–319.

Barzun, Jacques, and Graff, Henry F. *The Modern Researcher.* New York: Harbinger. 1961. pp. 347–348.

Bolles, Gary A. "Manual labor: What's up, doc?," *Network Computing*, 1991, 2(10):16–17.

Bolsky, Morris I. "Indexing," in *Better Scientific and Technical Writing.* Englewood Cliffs, N.J.: Prentice Hall. 1988. pg. 94.

Bonura, Larry S. "Courses to help you with indexing," *Indexers & Indexing*, 1985, 1(1):1.

Bonura, Larry S. *Desktop Publisher's Dictionary.* Plano, Texas: Wordware Publishing, 1989.

Bonura, Larry S. "Indexing: learned skill," *Indexers & Indexing*, 1985, 1(1):2.

Borko, Harold, and Bernier, Charles L. *Indexing Concepts and Methods.* New York: Academic Press. 1978.

British Standards Institution. *British Standard Recommendations for Preparing Indexes to Books, Periodicals and Other Documents.* BS 3700. London, England: BSI. 1988.

Brockmann, R. John. "Indexes," in *Writing Better Computer User Documentation: From Paper to Online.* New York: John Wiley. 1986. pp. 193–198.

Buchanan, Brian. *Glossary of Indexing Terms.* Hamden, Conn.: Shoestring Press. 1976.

Burnhill, P., Hartley, J., and Davies, L. "Typographic decision making: The layout of indexes," *Applied Ergonomics*, 1977, 8(1):35–39.

Butcher, Judith. "Indexes," in *Copy-Editing: The Cambridge Handbook*. Cambridge, England: Cambridge University Press. pp. 131–145.

Campbell, D.J. "Making your own indexing system in science and technology: classification and keyword system," *Aslib Proceedings*, 1963, 15(10):282–303.

Cleveland, Donald B., and Cleveland, Ana D. *Introduction to Indexing and Abstracting*. 2nd ed. Littleton, Colo.: Libraries Unlimited. 1990.

Coates, E. J. "Scientific and technical indexing," *The Indexer*, 1966, 5(1):27–34.

Collison, Robert L. "The elements of book indexing, part I," in *Training in Indexing: A Course of the Society of Indexers*. Cambridge, Mass.: The M.I.T. Press. pp. 14–27.

Collison, Robert L. "The elements of book indexing, part II," in *Training in Indexing: A Course of the Society of Indexers*. Cambridge, Mass.: The M.I.T. Press. pp. 28–39.

Collison, Robert L. *Indexes and Indexing*. 3rd ed. London: Ernest Benn Ltd. 1969.

Conference of Biological Editors. "Indexing," in *CBE Style Manual*. 3rd ed. Washington, D.C.: American Institute of Biological Sciences. pp. 109–204.

Coole, Sally. "How long should an index take?," *The Indexer*, 1972, 8(1):29–30.

Curry, Gene. "Indexing from the desktop—One writer's method." *Intercom*, 1993, 38(6):4–5.

Dinshaw, D. "Automatic generation of indexes for software manuals," in *Proceedings of the IEEE Professional Communication Society Conference*, 1983, pp. 177–183.

Drage, J.F. "User preferences in technical indexes," *The Indexer*, 1969, 6(4):151–155.

Fetters, Linda K. *A Guide to Indexing Software*. Port Aransas, Texas: American Society of Indexers. 1992.

Forrester, Michael A. "Hypermedia and indexing: identifying appropriate models from user studies." Unpublished paper. 1993.

Friedman, N. "Portable workbench for indexing documents," in *Proceedings: Next Decade in Information Technology*, 4th Jerusalem Conference on Information Technology, 1984, pp. 604–608.

Gould, A.M. "User preferences in published indexes," *Journal of the American Society for Information Science*, 1974, 25(5):279–286.

Grech, Christine. "Computer documentation doesn't pass muster," *PC/Computing*, 1992, 5(4):212, 214.

Grice, Roger A., and Ridgway, Lenore S. "Usability and hypermedia: Toward a set of usability criteria and measures," *Technical Communication*, 1993, 40(3):429–437.

Grodsky, Susan J. "Indexing technical communications: what, when, and how." *Technical Communication*, 1985, 32(2):26–30.

Hamilton, Geoffrey. "How to recognize a good index," *The Indexer*, 1976, 10(2):49–53.

Hewlett-Packard Company. "Indexing," in *Hewlett-Packard Writing Style Guide*. Palo Alto, Calif.: Hewlett-Packard Company. 1991. pp. 68–77.

Holmstrom, J. Edwin. "The indexing of scientific books," *The Indexer*, 1964, 4(4):123–131.

Holmstrom, J. Edwin. "Scientific and technical indexing, I," in *Training in Indexing: A Course of the Society of Indexers*. Cambridge, Mass.: The M.I.T. Press. pp. 109–127.

Holmstrom, J. Edwin. "Scientific and technical indexing, II," in *Training in Indexing: A Course of the Society of Indexers*. Cambridge, Mass.: The M.I.T. Press. pp. 128–141.

Horn, Robert E. *The Information Mapping Course for Writing Procedures, Policies, and Documentation*. Waltham, Mass.: Information Mapping, Inc. 1984.

Horton, William. "A quick (and not too dirty) fix for online documentation," *Technical Communication*, 1993, 40(3):517–521.

Knight, G. Norman. "Correction of index proofs," in *Training in Indexing: A Course of the Society of Indexers*. Cambridge, Mass.: The M.I.T. Press. pp. 176–187.

Knight, G. Norman. "Editing of indexes and their preparation for press," in *Training in Indexing: A Course of the Society of Indexers*. Cambridge, Mass.: The M.I.T. Press. pp. 167–175.

Knight, G. Norman. *Indexing, The Art of*. London: George Allen & Unwin. 1979.

Knight, G. Norman, ed. *Training in Indexing: A Course of the Society of Indexers*. Cambridge, Mass.: The M.I.T. Press. 1969.

Kochen, M., and Tagliacozzo, R. "A study of cross-referencing," *Journal of Documentation*, 1968, 24(3):173–191.

Langridge, Derek. "Subject headings," in *Training in Indexing: A Course of the Society of Indexers*. Cambridge, Mass.: The M.I.T. Press. pp. 75–85.

Law, M.D. "Introduction to book indexing." *The Indexer*, 1970, 7(2):46–48.

Lipetz, Ben-Ami. "The usefulness of indexes," *The Indexer*, 1989, 16(3):173–176.

Mackh, Georgia E., and Rew, Lois Johnson. "Using access aids to boost information retrieval," *Technical Communication*, 1991, 38(2):210–213.

Maddocks, Hugh C. *Generic Markup of Electronic Index Manuscripts*. Port Aransas, Texas: American Society of Indexers. 1988.

McColvin, L.R. "The purpose of indexing," *The Indexer*, 1958, 1(2):31–35.

Mitchell, Joan P. "Indexes," in *The New Writer: Techniques for Writing Well with a Computer*. Redmond, Wash.: Microsoft Press. 1987. pp. 226–227.

Morse, June. "How to recognize a good index," in *Stet! Tricks of the Trade for Writers and Editors*. Alexandria, Va.: Editorial Experts. 1986. pp. 214–217.

National Information Standards Organization. *Proposed American National Standard Guidelines for Indexes and Related Information Retrieval Devices*. NISO Z39.4-199x. Draft, version 4.1. 1993.

National Information Standards Organization. *Electronic Manuscripts: Preparation and Markup*. ANSI/NISO Z39.59. Bethesda, Md.: NISO. 1988

O'Neill, Carol L., and Ruder, Avima. "Indexing, freelance," in *The Complete Guide to Editorial Freelancing*. New York: Dodd, Mead. 1974. pp. 128–167.

Open Software Foundation. "Indexes," in *OSF Style Guide*. Cambridge, Mass.: Open Software Foundation. 1991. pp. 3-29 to 3-37.

Pakin, Sandra. "Preparing an index." *Sandra Pakin & Associates Folio*. Winter 1978.

Rada, Roy. *Hypertext: From text to expertext*. London: McGraw-Hill. 1991.

Richman, Jordan, and Richman, Vita. "To index or not to index! That's the question!" *PMA Newsletter*, 1993, 11(1):5, 9–11.

Ridehalgh, Nan. "The design of indexes," *The Indexer*, 1985, 14(3):165–174.

Seal, Alan. "Indexes from a user's viewpoint," *The Indexer*, 1984, 14(2):111–113.

Sencindiver, Martha. "Taking the mystery out of indexing," *Intercom*, 1991, 37(5):3–4.

Simpkins, Jean. "Assessing indexes," *The Indexer*, 1985, 14(3):179–180.

Simpkins, Jean. "How the publishers want it to look," *The Indexer*, 1990, 17(1):41–42.

Soergel, Dagobert. *Indexing Languages and Thesauri: Construction and Maintenance*. New York: Melville Publishing Company. 1974.

Software Engineering Technical Committee of the IEEE Computer Society. *IEEE Standard for Software User Documentation*. IEEE Std 1063-1987. New York: IEEE. 1988.

Specter, Lincoln. "Documentary," *Texas Computer Currents*, 1989, 1(5):31.

Spiker, Sina. *Indexing Your Book: A Practical Guide for Authors*. Madison, Wis.: University of Wisconsin Press. 1964.

Stirk, Jean. "User approaches to indexes," *The Indexer*, 1988, 16(2):75–78.

Thornton, John L. "Medical indexing," in *Training in Indexing: A Course of the Society of Indexers*. Cambridge, Mass.: The M.I.T. Press. pp. 142–151.

Travis, I.L., and Fidel, R. "Subject analysis," *Annual Review of Information Science and Technology*, 1982, 17:123–157.

University of Chicago Press. *Chicago Guide to Preparing Electronic Manuscripts for Authors and Publishers*. Chicago: University of Chicago Press. 1987.

University of Chicago Press. "Indexes," in *The Chicago Manual of Style*. Chicago: University of Chicago Press. pp. 511–557.

Wellisch, Hans H. *Indexing and Abstracting: An International Bibliography*. Santa Barbara, Calif.: ABC-Clio. 1980.

Wellisch, Hans H. *Indexing from A to Z*. New York: H.W. Wilson. 1991.

Wicklen, S.I. "The typography of indexes," *The Indexer*, 1(2):36–41.

B

See also

For more information

Index-learning turns no student pale,
Yet holds the eel of science by the tail.
— Alexander Pope, *The Dunciad*

Overview

This appendix provides names and addresses for the
following sources of indexing information:

- Organizations
- Publications
- Continuing education
- Seminars
- Software
- Online services

Organizations

American Society of Indexers (ASI)
P.O. Box 386
Port Aransas TX 78373
512/749-4052

Australian Society of Indexers (AusSI)
GPO Box 1251L
Melbourne, Victoria 3001 Australia

Indexing and Abstracting Society of Canada (IASC)
PO Box 744
Station F
Toronto, ON, Canada M4Y 2N6

National Federation of Abstracting and Information Services (NFAIS)
1429 Walnut St.
Philadelphia PA 19102
215/563-2406

Society of Indexers (SI)
16 Green Rd.
Birchington, Kent
CT7 9JZ UK

Publications

The Indexer—Free subscription comes with membership in the American Society of Indexers.

Key Words—A free subscription comes with membership in the American Society of Indexers.

Continuing education

The following institution offers structured, accredited courses in indexing:

U.S. Department of Agriculture Graduate School
Correspondence Programs
Room 1114, South Agriculture Building
14th Street and Independence Ave. S.W.
Washington DC 20250
202/720-7123

Seminars

The following companies offer seminars in indexing:

American Society of Indexers
P.O. Box 386
Port Aransas TX 78373
515/749-4052

National Federation of Abstracting and Information Services (NFAIS)
1429 Walnut Street
Philadelphia PA 19102
215/563-2406

Comtech Services, Inc.
710 N. Kipling, Suite 400
Denver CO 80215
303/232-7586

EEI
66 Canal Center Plaza, Suite 200
Alexandria VA 22314-5507
703/683-7453

Publishing Program
The University of Chicago
Center for Continuing Studies
5835 Kimbark Ave.
Chicago Il 60637-1608
312/702-1724

Skill Dynamics
An IBM Company
1000 N.W. 51st St.
Boca Raton FL 33432
602/799-7168

Society for Technical Communication
Seminars Program
901 N. Stuart St.
Suite 904
Arlington VA 22203-1854
703/522-4114

Solutions, Inc.
274 Main Street
Reading MA 01867
617/942-1610

UCLA Extension
10995 Le Conte Ave.
Los Angeles CA 90024-2883
310/825-9971

Word Workers
P.O. Box 831038
Richardson TX 75083-1038
214/907-9673

Indexing software

There are several indexing programs available for most operating systems. An excellent reference is *A Guide to Indexing Software* by Linda Fetters, which is available from the American Society of Indexers. Here are some of the most commonly used programs and their sources.

CINDEX (PC)

Indexing Research
P.O. Box 18609
Rochester NY 14618-0109
716/461-5530

IndexAid (PC)

Santa Barbara Software Products
1400 Dover Rd.
Santa Barbara CA 93103
805/963-4886

Indexer's Assistant (PC)

Omega Electronics
P.O. Box 294
Oswego NY 13126
315/342-1741

Indexit (PC)

Graham Conley Press
1936 E. Belmont
Tempe AZ 85284

INDEXX (PC)

Norman Swartz
1053 Ridley Dr.
Burnaby, BC, Canada V5A 2N7
604/420-7454

In>Sort (Macintosh and PC)

Kensa Software
P.O. Box 4415
Northbrook IL 60065
708/559-0297

LS/Index (UNIX)

Language System Inc.
944 Kensington Ave.
Plainfield NJ 07060
908/932-4170

MACREX (PC)

Bayside Indexing Services
P.O. Box 3051
Daly City CA 94015-0051
415/756-0821

NLCindex (PC)

Newberry Library
60 W. Walton St.
Chicago IL 60610
312/943-9090

wINDEX (PC)

Watch City Software
24 Harris St.
Waltham MA 02154
617/893-0514

Electronic services

If you use Bitnet or Internet, INDEX-L is an excellent and well-established electronic conference venue for indexers.

INDEX-L is a group that provides a forum for aspiring and professional indexers to share information and ideas relating to the intellectual, philosophical, and technical aspects of indexing.

To join, send the following message to listserv@bingvmb.bitnet:

    Subscribe INDEX-L Jane Doe

where Jane Doe is your real first and last name.

C

Glossary

Words defined

Marking text constitutes nothing more than the hollow
mechanics of indexing; the true demands lie in recognizing
appropriate passages to include, and that can't be learned
without years of experience.
— Rick Altman in "Indexing Software for Ventura
Publisher" in *Computer Currents*

Overview

This appendix contains a selected glossary of indexing
terms.

analytical index—An index that uses subheadings to classify the concepts contained in its subject entries in accordance with the text.

complex entry—An entry in which there are subheadings when references are numerous enough for systematic grouping.

compound heading—A heading comprising two or more elements (with or without connecting hyphen), each of which could stand alone with its own meaning: air-sea rescue, Henry VIII, John o'Groat's, air-to-surface missiles.

cross-reference—A direction from one heading (or any of its subheadings) to another heading.

cumulative index—An index comprising entries from multiple volumes in a set of books. Also called a *master index*. Often the index to the final volume will not appear separately but will be merged in the cumulative index.

entry—A unit of the index consisting of a heading (and qualifying expression, if any) with at least one reference to the location of the item in the text (or else with a *see* reference), together with any subheadings and their relevant references. The presence of subheadings, when references are numerous enough for systematic grouping, constitutes a complex entry.

heading—The words or symbols selected from, or based on, an item in the text, arranged in alphabetical or other chosen order.

index—An indicator or pointer to the position of required information. It is a systematic guide to the text of any reading matter, comprising a series of entries with headings arranged in alphabetical order or other chosen order and with references to show where each item indexed is located.

indexing—(noun) The compilation of an index; (adjective) pertaining to such a compilation.

inversion—A compound heading (or subheading) having the actual order of its elements reversed, in order that the second part may supply the key word: The inversion of *word-by-word alphabetizing* is *alphabetizing, word-by-word.*

key word—The initial word of a heading or a subheading (provided the subheadings are arranged alphabetically).

letter-by-letter alphabetizing—An alphabetizing method that treats the groups as single entities alphabetized all through, letter-by-letter:

North Carolina
North-easter (wind)
Northfield, Vermont
North Pole
Northumbria
North Vernon, Indiana

line-by-line format—Format where all subheadings are arranged in columnar form under the heading:

page numbers
  bold facing 54
  format of 60
  recording 43
  separating, with commas 60
  strings of, avoiding 56

line wrap—An index line that continues beyond one typeset line. Also called *turnover line.*

locator—The number of the page, folio, section, or paragraph, or other specific indication where the item or subject indexed is to be found in the text. Also called a *reference.*

main heading—A description sometimes used for a heading in contradistinction to subheading.

master index—An index comprising entries from multiple volumes in a set of books. Also called a *cumulative index*. Often the index to the final volume will not appear separately but will be merged in the cumulative index.

modification—A descriptive word added to a simple or compound heading to differentiate terms.

qualified heading—A simple or compound heading with descriptive words added, following punctuation or parentheses:

state (computer condition)
state (governmental entity)

The second instance is sometimes described as *modification*.

reference—The number of the page, folio, section, or paragraph, or other specific indication where the item or subject indexed is to be found in the text. Also called a *locator*.

run-on format—Format where all subheadings are arranged to follow one another in ordinary paragraph form and spread over the entire column:

page numbers: bold facing 54; format of 60; recording 43; separating, with commas 60; strings of, avoiding 56

see **reference**—A direction from one heading (or subheading), after which there are no page or other references, to an alternative heading, under which all the relevant references to an item in the text are collected.

see also **reference**—A direction from one heading (or subheading) to any additional heading(s), under which further relevant references to an item in the text are to be found.

simple heading—A heading consisting of a single word or a word with a hyphenated prefix or a suffix which alone would either have no meaning or have a different meaning.

subheading—The words or symbols under which references in a complex entry are specifically located:

magazines (heading)
  history of (subheading)
  titles of
    capitalization rules for (sub-subheading)
    title of, italicized

subject—A unit of concept found in, or derived from, the material indexed. The unit concept may be found or expressed as a thematic topic, a name, a date, the first line of a poem, the title of a work, an expression coined to given the gist of the material indexed, restrictions, and so on.

text—All the reading matter in a book (and its illustrations) other than its index.

turnover line—An index line that continues beyond one typeset line. Also called *line wrap*.

word-by-word alphabetization—An alphabetical arrangement of compound headings and compound subheadings where they are treated as separate words, each alphabetized in turn:

North Carolina
North Pole
North Vernon, Indiana
North-easter (wind)
Northumbria
Northfield, Vermont

D

Sample indexes

Show me what you mean

A good index records every pertinent statement made
within the body of the text. The key word here is *pertinent*.
— *The Chicago Manual of Style*, 13th Edition

Objectives

This appendix presents examples of several kinds of
indexes:

- Concordance
- Permuted title
- Master
- MIL-SPEC
- Combination
- Edited
- Notes
- Special cases

Concordance-type index

In this type of index, words are arranged alphabetically, but with little or no modification or analysis.

A

short, program 9-6, 9-10, 9-11
accesses, memory 6-8
accesses, partial memory 6-13
accessing arrays 6-8
actual arguments 8-3
adjustable arrays 8-2
algebraic simplification 2-10
algorithms, parallelism of 1-3, 5-7
alias, defined D-1
aliases, hidden 9-2, 9-4
allocation of registers 2-4
alternate entry, routine 8-2
alternate exists, loop 6-5
ANSI FORTRAN 77 Standard 9-2, 9-6
antidependency 7-4
apparent dependency 4-5, 5-8, 9-9
apparent recurrence 3-7, 9-8, 9-9, 9-10, B-9
arguments, actual 8-3
arguments, dummy 8-1, 8-3, 9-2, B-13
array compression C-2
array expansion C-2
array I/O, implicit B-13
array index, odd leading 6-12
array merging C-2
array strides, even 6-11
array strides, odd 6-11
array, accessing 6-8
array, adjustable 8-2
array, dummy 9-6
array, in EQUIVALENCE 3-7, 4-5
array, promoting 7-4
array, storage of 6-7
ASAP 1-3
ASSIGN_LOCK directive B-4, B-5
ASSIGN statement 2-12
assigned GOTO statement 3-7
assignment substitution 2-7
assignment, elimination of redundant 2-7, 2-11
Automatic Self-Allocating Processor 1-3

B

backward dependency 3-8, 3-9, 3-11, 4-6, 4-7
balanced tree 2-4, 2-5
bank conflict 6-10, 6-12, 6-13
bank, memory 6-8, 6-9, 6-12
basic-block level 1-2
BEGIN_ORDER directive B-4
BEGIN_SECTION directive B-5
BEGIN_TASKS directive 4-8, B-6
binary search procedure 5-2
binary vector operator C-6
boundary value test 6-6

Permuted index

In the permuted index the alphabetical words appear in the middle of the page, flanked on either side by words appearing before and after the entry.

Master index

This index contains entries for multiple volumes that comprise a single product. Also called a *cumulative index*.

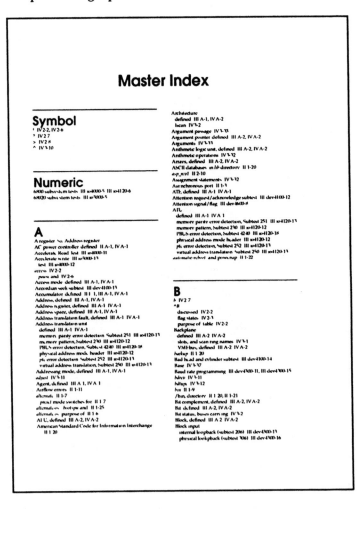

MIL-SPEC index

This index conforms to the standards required by United States military specifications.

DOCUMENT PREPARATION GUIDE	CHAPTER	Index
	PAGE	I-3
	DATE	May 1991

SUBJECT INDEX TO DOCUMENT PREPARATION GUIDE

Note: Except for Chap. 1 and Appendix C, this index refers to sections rather than to pages

Time periods 6.7.11, 6.7.12
Titles of headings 6.7.14, 6.7.18, p C-8
Topographical names 6.7.4
Trade names 6.7.13
Tribes, nationalities, races 6.7.6
With punctuation, 6.7.18
Caption (see Illustrations)
Category Distribution (see Standard Distribution System)
Caution Notes (see also Notice)
  Applied Technology
  Internal Use Only 3.2.1.6
  Patent 3.2.1.6
  Preliminary Information
Chart Book
  Definition Chap 1
  Preparation 4.4.13
Chemical Notations
  Atomic numbers 6.16.3
  Chemical equations 6.16.11
  Elements 6.16.13
  Formulas, 6.16.3
  Greek letters 6.16.14
  In tables 4.5.19
  Ionic charge, 6.16.3
  Isotopes, 6.16.12
  Italics 6.16.6
  Mass numbers 6.16.3
  Molality, 6.16.5
  Molarity 6.16.5
  Normality 6.16.5
  Nuclear reactions 6.16.9
  Numbers 6.16.3
  Oxidation states 6.16.4
  Percent composition, 6.16.7
  Spelling 6.16.2
  Superscripts and subscripts, 6.16.8
  Symbols 6.16.13
  Thermodynamic notation, 6.16.10
Cities and States
  Use without states 6.2.3.1
Classification
  Category Chap 1, 3.2.1.3, 3.2.1.4, 4.1.1.2, 4.1.4
  Markings 3.2.1.2, 3.1.2.3, 3.2.1.4 4.1.1.2, 4.1.4
  Determination Chap 1, 3.3.1
    Policy 2.2.1
    Release approval, 3.4
    Original representative Chap 1

Illustrations, 4.4.2
Level, Chap 1, 3.2.1.2, 3.2.1.4, 4.1.1.2, 4.1.4, 4.1.6
Markings, 3.2.1.2, 3.2.1.3, 3.2.1.4, 4.1.1.2, 4.1.4 4.1.6
of Information Chap 1
Officer Chap 1, 3.1.3, 3.3.3
Preliminary review, 3.1.3
Review (see Classification Determinations) Chap 1, 3.1.3
Classified
  Data, reference citations to p C-3
  Information, Chap 1
  Page numbers 5.4.2
  Titles 4.6.1.1
Classified Matter Protection Guide, Chap 1, 2.2.1
Classifier
  Authorized, Chap 1, 3.3.1
  Declassifier, Chap 1
  Derivative, Chap 1, 3.3.1, 4.1.1.2, 4.1.4
  Original Chap 1
Clause
  Main, 6.6.4.1 6.6.5
  Nonrestrictive, 6.6.4.4
  Restrictive, 6.6.4.4
Cliches, 6.9
Collective Nouns, 6.10
Colon use of, 6.6.6 6.7.19
Color Printing (see also Reproduction), 4.4.5, 5.6
Comma, use of 6.6.4
  Introductory elements 6.6.4.2
  Items in a series 6.6.4.3
  Main clauses, 6.6.4.1
  Miscellaneous uses, 6.6.4.4
  Parenthetical expressions, 6.6.4.4
  Series 6.6.4.3
Completion Report
  Definition, Chap 1
  Description, 2.3.7
  Release approval, 3.4.9
Composition
  Percent 6.16.7
Compound Adjectives 6.5.2
Compound Words (see Compounding and Hyphenation)
Compounding and Hyphenation (see also Hyphenation)
  Compound words 6.5.3
  Hyphen with prefixes and suffixes 6.5.1
  Hyphens with unit modifiers 6.5.2
  Word division 6.3.2

Combination index

This index combines several different types of indexes into one: a grid spacing index, a parts number index, and a subject index.

Subjects

A

Accessories	D-42, D-46, I-34, I-56, I-79
	I-83, G-26, N-74, N-75, N-76, N-77
	N-78, N-79
Accessory Tool	M-14
Accessory Tooling	M-12, M-13
Application Information	I-38
Assembly Equipment	O-1
Stackable Socket	B-18
Assembly Kit	L-40
Assembly Nest	O-13

Edited index

This is an example of an edited index.

Index

A

a command (archiver) 7 3
a option (linker) 8-5
A_DIR 3-9 3 10 8
absolute output module 8-6
absolute sections 2 7 4 19
align 4 10 4-18
alignment 4-10 4-18 8-25 to
allocation 4-24 8-24
alignment 8-25
binding 8-25
data memory 8-25
default algorithm 8 28
GROUP option, 8-27
named memory 8-26 to
program memory 8-25,
alternate directories
assembler 3-9
C_DIR 8-8
linker 8-8
archive libraries 3-9 4-49 7; 8-8 8-12
8-15
archiver 7-1
examples 7-5
the development flow 7 2
input 7-1
invocation 7
options 7
output 7-1
arithmetic operators 3-21
array definitions A-23
ASCII character set F-1
asect 2-4 22 4-5 4-19 4-50
asg 4-14 6-6

assembler 3-1 28
character strings 3 16 3-17
constants 3 14 3-15
cross-reference listings 3 27
directives 4-1 4-17
error messages D-1 D-6
expressions 3-20
the development flow 3-2
invocation 3 3
macros 6-1 6-22
output 3-24
overview 3-1
relocation, 2-19 2-28
section program counters 2-7
sections 2-4 2-22
sections directives
asect 2-4 2-7
bss 2-4,
data 2-4,
sect 2-4
text 2-4
usect 2-4
source listings 3-24
source statement format 3-12 3-13
symbols 2-21
assembler directive/symbolic debugging directive/ sym B 10
assembler directives, 4-1 to 4-17
conditional assembly
else 4-13 4-42
endif 4 13 4-42
if 4-13 4-42
sections directives
asect 4-5 1-49
bss 4-5 4-24
data 4-5 4-30

Notes in indexes

These are examples of index notes used to inform readers of special information, such as volume identification in master indexes or typographic variations in locators to indicate specific items.

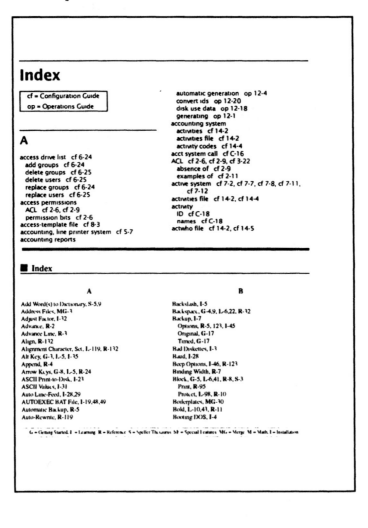

Index

■ Index

Special cases

These indexes show how clip art is handled and how control keys are managed in two different indexes.

Clip-Art Symbol Index

Description	No	Page	Description	No.	Page
A			Animals continued		
			Eagle (Emblematic)	3651	3-40
Abacus	3925	3-12	Sheep (One)	1137	3-6
Adding Machine	5097	3-12	Ape (Baboon)	4450	3-6
Tape	3258	3-12	Arm in Sling	2800	3-55
Airplanes			Arrowheads		2-17
Biplane	3682	3-3	Arrows		2-10
Fighter	2017	3-3	3-D		2-12
Fighter (WWII)	15040	1-4	Multidirectional		2-12
Paper	4061	1-61	Ax	4457	3-66
Ampersand (&)	2669	1-45	Axes (X and Y)		6-4
Anchor	1052	1-57			
Anchor	4129	1-57	**B**		
Animals					
Ape (Baboon)	4450	3-6	Baboon	4450	3-6
Bear	1011	3-6	Badge, Sheriff's	2802	3-23
Bear, Teddy	4215	4-2	Ball Bearings	3155	3-72
Dog Puppy	2278	3-6	Banners		2-13
Dog Running	4200	3-6	Baseball	4465	3-62
Dog Terrier	2272	3-6	Baseball		3-62
Dog Tired	10692	3-6	Bathtub	4411	3-35

WordStar Index

^QZ (Scroll down continuously) 66 1.19 **236**
^Q 0-9 (Cursor to place marker) 1.19 **166**

R

R (run a DOS command) 234
^R or PgUp (Scroll up one screen) 139 **236**
^R (Repeat answer), 228
Ragged right text 39-40 **178**
Random access memory (RAM) **186** 127
README information xxx
Read variable for merge printing (RV) 190-191
Records 92 94 **142**
Reforming text See Aligning
Renaming files
   at Opening Menu (F) 2.31
   while editing (^KE) 161 **231**
Repeating commands (^QQ) 231
Replacing See Finding and replacing
Restore deleted text See Undo and unerase
Right-justified text 39 **178**

RM (Right margin) 39 **183**
Root directory 216 **321**
RP (Repeat printing) 225
RR (Embed ruler line) 79 **233**
Ruler line 27 35-36 **232-234**
   displaying (^OT) 232
   embedded (^OO or RR) 76 78-79 **233**
   from text (^OF) 233-234
Running a DOS command (R or ^KF) 2.14
RV (Read variable) 97-98 190-191

S

^S (Cursor left one character) 28 **139**
Saving blocks and writing to separate file (^KW) **123**
   161 235
Saving files
   and printing (^PrtSc) 2.35
   and quitting WordStar (^KX) 235
   and resuming editing (^KS) 235
   and returning to Opening Menu (^KD) 2.1 **235**

E

Sample indexing style guide

Design for consistency

So essential did I consider an index to be to every book that
I proposed to bring a bill into Parliament to deprive an
author who published a book without an index of the
privilege of copyright, and moreover, to subject him for his
offense to a pecuniary penalty.
— John Campbell, *Lives of the Chief Justices of England*

Objectives

In this appendix you will learn:

- How to develop a style for your index

Index defined

An index is a retrieval device, an access aid. But it is not a list of terms or ideas, like a table of contents or a concordance, which is an alphabetical list of words in a document with their immediate contexts. Neither a table of contents nor a concordance systematically analyzes the topics.

An index is a systematic topical analysis alphabetically arranged or arranged by function, command, procedure, or topic. It is a reader's most important map for locating information in a document that is read in a random-access style.

An index is one of the most important parts of a good technical document. It allows readers fast, random access to the contents of your document. A good index saves the reader time in locating information, saves support costs, and improves user satisfaction.

Documents requiring indexes

Your document needs an index to decreases the time that the reader spends locating information. All documents that are used as a reference and have more than 32 pages should have an index. Shorter documents may also need an index. Quick references may not need an index if the reader can easily find information without an index. Sets of documents should have a master index, which is an index of the information in all the documents in the set.

Index length

Index length depends upon the length of the document and the complexity of the information it contains. A typical density for an index is five entries per page. Each reference counts as an entry.

Index entries

An index entry is a unit of the index consisting of a heading with at least one reference to the location of the item in the text together with any subheadings and their relevant references. An entry helps the reader locate the information the reader is searching for. Therefore, create an index entry for anything that the reader is likely to want to refer to. Use terminology that the reader is likely to look up.

What to index

What you index depends on the content and scope of the document. But consider indexing the following items:

- Acronyms
- Alternate names and common synonyms
- Appendix information
- Command names
- Error conditions and messages
- Examples
- Figures
- Glossary terms
- Introductory information
- Keyboard keys
- Measurements
- Menu options
- Overviews
- Proper names
- Screen selections
- Restrictions
- Special characters
- Tables
- Tasks

Acronyms

Index acronyms under the abbreviation, spelling out the name after the acronym if the name is generally known. For example:

MS-DOS (Microsoft Disk Operating System), 32, 65

Also index the acronym under the spelled-out name, if it is generally known. For example, also enter "MS-DOS" under the entry

Microsoft Disk Operating System (MS-DOS), 32, 65

Alternate names and common synonyms

Index alternate names, common synonyms, and terms the reader may be familiar with from other sources. For example, index "concatenate" and provide "*see* concatenate" references for other, common terms:

join, *see* concatenate
merge, *see* concatenate
append, *see* concatenate
combine, *see* concatenate

Try to anticipate what entries readers will attempt to find based on their experience with similar products and industry standards.

Appendix information

It is preferred that you index information in the appendix if that information can be expected to be searched by readers.

Command names

Index all command names, placing the command in the typeface used in your document.

Error conditions and messages

Index error conditions under the name of the hardware or software involved. For example:

displays, problems with
configuration utility, problems with

Also, index informative messages under:

error messages
messages

Examples

Index examples if the information contained in the example is significant beyond the information found in the supporting text.

Figures

At minimum, create one reference to each figure. Because figures often contain large amounts of detailed and varied information, you are encouraged to include several references for each figure.

Glossary terms

While glossaries do not have to be indexed, sometimes it helps the reader if the glossary is indexed. It would be a good habit to index all definitions, those in the glossary as well as in text. If the definition appears in the text and glossary, each with slight variations in meaning, you might show the differences in the index by choosing a term that is used consistently to define each. For example:

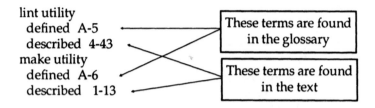

In this example, each time a topic in the glossary was indexed, the term *defined* was used. When the same topic was described in text, the term *described* was used.

Introductory information

Index introductory information if the information contained in the introductory pages is significant.

Keyboard keys

Index keyboard keys by name. Also index by key cap if the key name appears as a keycap in the text. For example:

Enter key, 145, 290
(Enter), 145, 290

Measurements

Index measurements if they are important to readers, such as for default values, options, and restrictions.

Menu options

Index all menu options.

> Left Page Header, 66, 78–84
> Right Page Header, 67, 78–84

Overviews

Index information in overviews.

Proper names

Index proper names that the reader might wish to look up. Identify with a descriptive word or phrase, in parentheses, if necessary. For example:

> Pascal, Blaise (mathematician), 56

Restrictions

The reader must be able to find all restrictions and the index should make the reader aware of them. Do not just list the restriction. Be sure to describe it, too. There are several types of restrictions that should be entered:

- Sets of rules
- Default values or options
- Warnings
- Cautions
- Notes

Screen selections

Index screen selections if the information contained in the screen is significant.

Special characters

Index special characters under the character and under the spelled-out name. Place a description of the special character in parentheses after the characters and the characters in parentheses after the spelled-out name. For example:

! (repeat command), 44
& (background operation), 68
+ (Boolean operator), 109
repeat command (!), 44
background operation (&), 68
Boolean operator (+), 109

Index terms that begin with a special character under the character and alphabetically under the term. For example:

Symbols
%include, 56

I
%include, 56

Tables

At minimum, create one reference to each table. Because tables often contain large amounts of detailed and varied information, you are encouraged to include several references for each table.

Tasks

If your document contains tasks, index them. For example:

reports, printing
printing reports

What not to index

Do not index passing references to a subject.

Creating subentries

Create a subentry when an entry has more than three page references or when the use of subentries decreases the time to locate information.

Keep subentries as short as possible.

Use up to two levels of subentries, for a total of three levels. For example:

Do not use:

    book
        creating, 45
        saving, as ASCII text, 134
        saving, to different drive, 56

Instead, use:

    book
        creating, 45
        saving
            as ASCII text, 134
            to different drive, 56

Creating cross-references

Use cross-references to direct the user to:

- A word that has one or more synonyms
- An entry that is alphabetized under a different letter
- Related entries

Place *see* and *see also* in italic and lowercase them. Do not end *see* and *see also* references with periods.

See

Use the *see* cross-reference for synonyms and for entries under a different letter.

Use the most familiar version of the term as the accepted term and put page references with that term. Use *see* to refer to the accepted term. For example:

books, 56
documents. *see* books

Use *see* to refer to an entry that is alphabetized under a different letter. For example:

printing books. *see* books, printing

See also

Use *see also* to refer to a related entry. The current entry must contain at least one page reference. For example:

books, 56. *see also* file management

Connecting entries

Use connecting words, such as *the, of, with,* and *and,* in entries when they make the entry easier to understand and to read. For example:

    configuration, advanced method
       getting help with, 16-3
       problems with, 12-4 to 12-8
       starting, 14-2

Formatting the index

Use the following guidelines to format your index. Although the word processor, page-formatting system, desktop-publishing package, or electronic-publishing system used may not be able to meet all the recommendations, try to incorporate as many of the guidelines as possible.

Type size and style

It is preferable to print the index in 8-point type. You have two other options:

- Use the same type size as the body text.
- Use a type size not more than 2 point sizes smaller than the text.

Print the headings between letter groups, called *separators* or *letter headings,* in boldface type that is 2 point sizes larger than the type size of the index text.

Print *see* and *see also* in italic type.

Capitalize only proper nouns and words that are capitalized in the text. For example, capitalize acronyms and commands that are capitalized in the text.

General format

Use a two-column format for small-format books, and a three-column format for large-format books.

Indent subentries one em space under entries. For example:

indexes
  definition of, 31
  master, 74, 78
  software for, 110

Make the indent for line wraps, also called *turnover lines,* one em space greater than the indent for the number of subentry levels. For example:

date, setting and changing,
    3-34 to 3-35
disk drives
  flexible, 6-8
    storing, 9-10
    magnetism and, 3-1
  hard, 4-6
  removing, 6-8 to 6-9

Column breaks

Make columns end at the end of an entry and its subentries, whenever possible. When subentries continue to the next column, print the main entry followed by "(continued)" at the top of the next column. For example:

books (continued)
  printing, 34

When a second level of subentries continues to the next
column, print the main entry and the subentry, each
followed by *(continued)*, at the top of the next column. For
example:

> books (continued)
>> printing (continued)
>>> graphics, 56
>>> spreadsheets, 88
>>> word processing, 89

Letter headings

Letter headings are the headings between each letter
section of an index. Use a letter heading called *Symbols* for
entries that begin with special (nonalphanumeric)
characters. Print the *Symbols* letter heading at the
beginning of the index.

Place numerals in the letter heading of the number as if
spelled out.

Sort order

Sort entries letter by letter for words, ignoring connecting
words such as *of*, *with*, and *and*. Sort numerals in
alphabetical order. Sort nonalphanumeric characters in
ascending order of their ASCII equivalent.

Sort letters alphabetically, ignoring capitalization and word
breaks. Sort the capital letter after the lowercase letter
when entries differ only in capitalization.

An example of sort orders:

> image, 4
> %include, 99
> include, 234
> INCLUDE, 4–12
> invert, 30, 37

Punctuation

Use a comma before the first page reference and between all subsequent references. For example:

> change bars, 5, 7, 65
> feedback, 107

Use an en dash to indicate a range of pages when the folio does not include a chapter number. For example:

> time, changing, 34–36

Use the word *to* to indicate a range of pages when the folio includes the chapter number. For example:

> time, changing, 9-34 to 9-35

For entries that direct the reader to another entry, print the entry, a period, the word *see* (in italic), and the entry the reader is directed to. For example:

> cards. *see* boards

Practices to avoid

Here are some caveats to be aware of:

Tables and figures

Do not emphasize the page references for tables and figures. For example, do not print page references for tables and figures in italic.

Page ranges

With chapter-page style numbering, do not abbreviate the page references when indicating a range of pages. Instead, use the word *to* to indicate a range. For example:

Do not use:

> time, changing, 8-34-35 or
> time, changing, 8-34-5

Instead, use:

> time, changing, 8-34 to 8-35

Page references

Do not split a page reference between lines. For example:

Do not use:

> time, changing and setting, 34-
>   35
> time, changing and setting, 8-
>   34 to 8-35

Instead, use:

> time, changing and
>   setting, 34-35
> time, changing and
>   setting, 8-34 to 8-35

Column style

Do not allow a main entry to print as the last entry in a column when the main entry has subentries. Print the main entry, followed by its subentries, at the top of the next column instead.

Do not start a column with a line of page references.

Do not end a column with a new letter heading, or with a new letter heading and one entry.

Letter headings

Do not combine letters of the alphabet as a single letter heading. For example:

Do not use:

J,K

Instead, use:

J
K

Do not list a letter heading when no entries appear for that letter heading. For example, do not use "K" for a letter heading when there are no entries that begin with "K."

Editing the index

Once the index is created, verify its accuracy with the following activities:

- Check that page references are correct and appear in ascending numerical order.
- Check that all *see* and *see also* references lead to entries that exist. All *see also* references should lead to new information, not the same information under a different entry.
- Check that the entries are in the proper sort order.
- Check for consistency in verb forms and noun forms.
- Check for consistent use of connecting words.
- Check that all sections of the document are indexed and that all sections are equally represented in the index.
- User-test the index to ensure that the entries are useful to your target audience.

Master indexes

Master indexes span multiple volumes. These indexes include entries from all the documents in a particular document set. Sets of documents should have a copy of the master index in all the volumes in the set. It is also acceptable to issue the index as a separate book, if necessary.

Format of master indexes

Include an abbreviation or a volume number to identify each volume that makes up the document set. Insert a space between the abbreviation or volume number and the page reference. Separate page references in different documents with a semicolon. For example:

networks, HWR 43; TNR 202-210
solving problems, IV 23-89

Provide a key to the abbreviations at the bottom of each index page.

Verifying a master index

Ensure that terminology is used consistently in every document in the set.

Check that all documents in the set are indexed and that they are equally represented.

Index

A

abbreviations 30
  index size and 120
  indexing 47, 59, 67
access routes, for online indexes 154
accessing hypertext documents 152
accounts, tracking 125
accuracy 30
  criteria for good index 26
  guidelines for determining 136
  indexer trait 12
  testing for 136
acknowledgments, not indexed 145
acronyms 59, 67
  analyzing topics and 47
  capitalizing 207
  style guide example 200
  Wheatley Medal criteria and 30
adjectives
  and noun compounds, not inverted 57
  in factoring 63
administrating index, chart 127
administration time, tracking 124
alphabetical subject indexes 15
alphabetizing 30, 58, 69–72
  see also chronological order
  accuracy of, checking for 136
  accuracy of, checking for, in indexing software 102
  cross-references, multiple 76
  editing for 132
  indexing software and 102
  letter-by-letter 70, 136
  order of 71, 130
  see references 78
  style guide example 209
  word-by-word 71, 136
American National Standards 159
American National Standards Institute 159

B

D

dedication, indexer trait 12
default values, indexing 66, 203
definitions, indexing 47, 66, 202
depth, of indexing
  evaluating for 26
  testing for 137
desktop publishing 90
  indexing with 99
diagrams
  locators for 88
  referencing 133
dingbats, alphabetizing 130

E

editing 129–134
  checklist for 132
  cross-references 82, 102
  index cards 94
  indexing software and 102
  sample 193
  style guide example 213
  time
    chart 127
    tracking 124
EEI, address 176
Electronic Manuscripts: Preparation and Markup 161
electronic publishing 90
  indexing with 99
electronic services 180
elements
  cross-references
    discussed 44
    illustrated 44
  discussed 42
  entries
    discussed 42
    illustrated 43
  locators
    discussed 43
    illustrated 43
  order of 130
elisions
  see also inclusive numbers; locators
  rules for using 87

G

M

N

O

P

Q

R

S

T

U

V

value, of book, index adds to 5
vocabulary control, online indexes and 150
volume numbers, in locators 43

W

warnings, indexing 47, 66, 203
Wheatley Medal, criteria for 30
when to index 144
wINDEX, address 180
word arrangement, for emphasis 62
word order 56
word processors, indexing with 99
word spaces, in alphabetizing 70
Word Workers, address 177
word-by-word alphabetizing 136
  see also alphabetizing; letter-by-letter alphabetizing
  discussed 71
  example 70
wording
  of text, faithfulness to 22–23
  variations in, editing for 132
writers
  as audiences 18
  as indexers 11

Z

Z39.4 159

Printed in the United States
205374BV00003BA/4/A